I0796198

RAFIQ AZAM

OLD DHAKA–NEW STORY
ARCHITECTURE IN BANGLADESH

RAFIQ AZAM

OLD DHAKA–NEW STORY
ARCHITECTURE IN BANGLADESH

Edited by
Rosa Maria Falvo

New York · Paris · London · Milan

dedication

The name Zannat is of Arabic origin, meaning "heaven," while Jasminum auriculatum is a flower species that is commonly called "jui" and often seen in celebrations throughout South Asia. Combined, they create the perfect name for my beautiful wife—Zannat Jui—whose presence in my life motivates me to navigate challenges peacefully, and to whom I dedicate this book.

CONTENTS

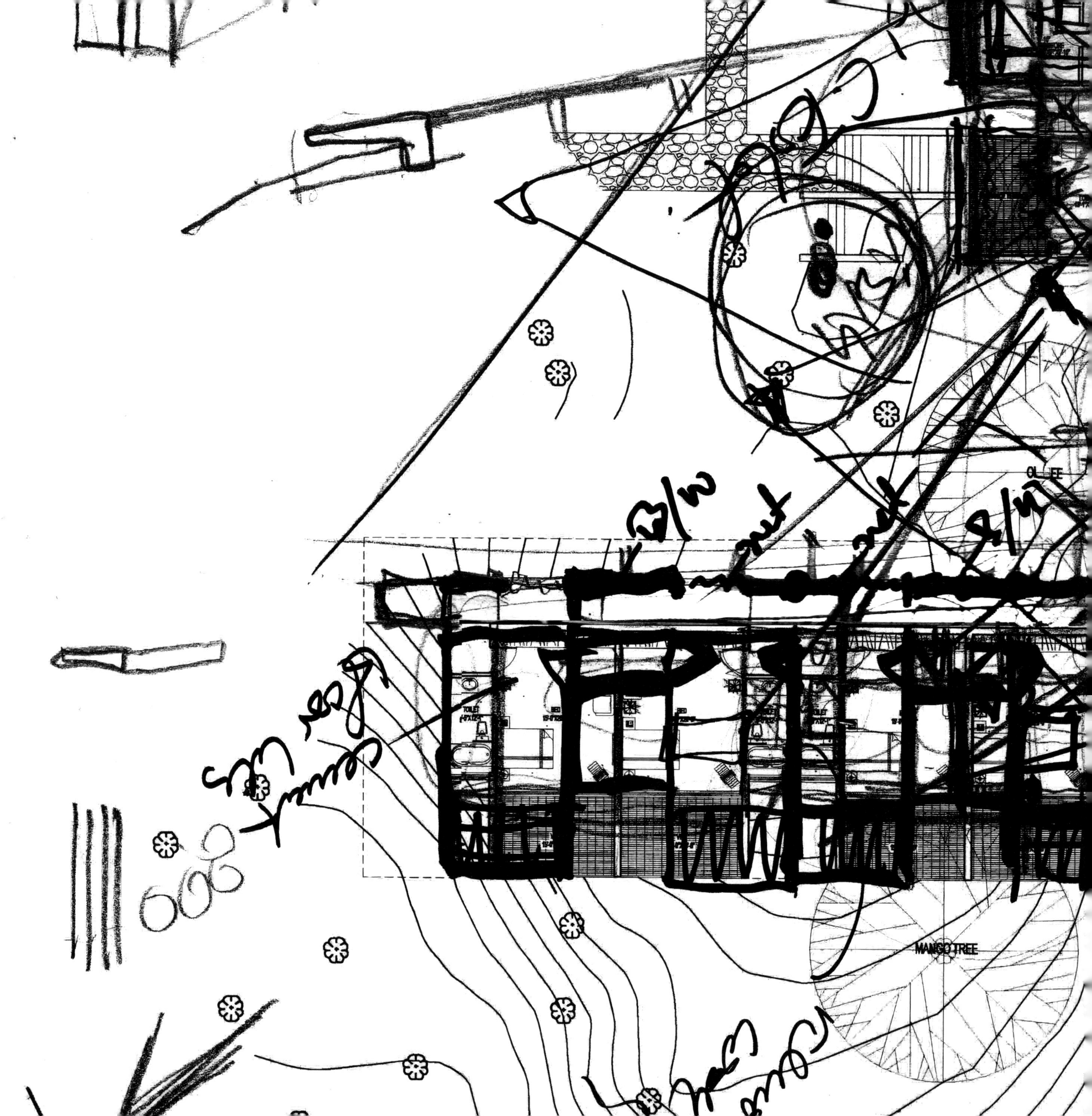
MANGO TREE

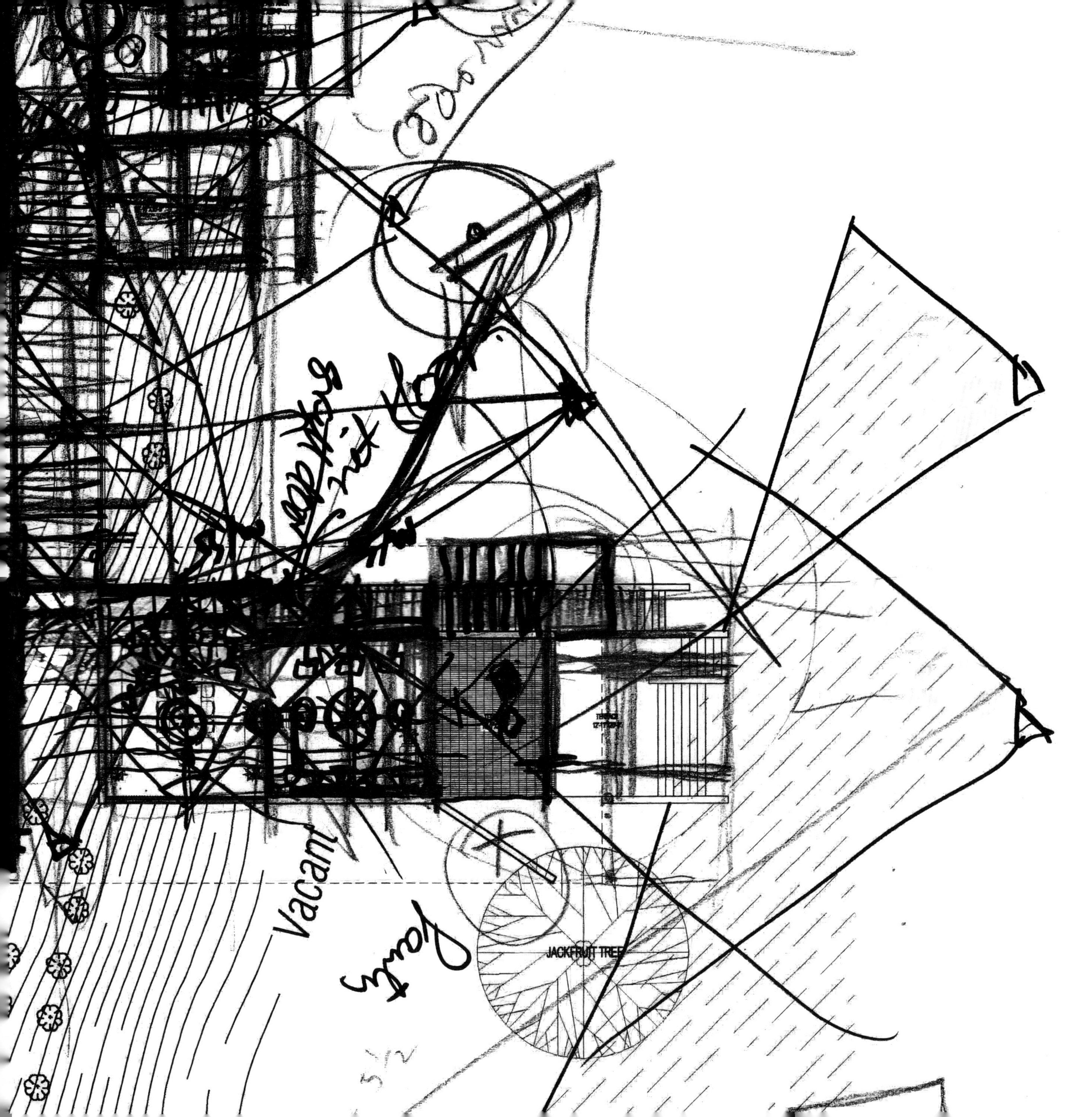

IN THE NAME OF MODERNITY

KENNETH B. FRAMPTON

tradition and innovation

The object of human knowledge is not strictly an object, it is the institution within human space and historical time, of artifacts, tools, services, institutions that those before us have thought needed and valued … This human legacy is never fully ours until we learn to alter it through our personal style.

John O'Neill, *The Communicative Body*, 1989

When I first saw the work of Rafiq Azam, I was impressed not only by his ability as a painter to capture the ineffable fluidity of water, but also by his capacity as an architect to reformulate the mid-rise, middle-class apartment building: as an assembly of vertically clustered dwelling units of reinforced concrete, framed construction, clad throughout in precision brickwork with exposed concrete floor slabs. This "brutalist" aesthetic resembled the "towered" clusters of Louis Kahn's Richards Medical Research Building, Goddard Laboratories (1957–1964), designed for the University of Pennsylvania. Around the same time, on the advice of the prestigious Bengali architect, Muzharul Islam, Kahn was commissioned by the Bangladesh government to design the National Parliament in Dhaka—*Jatiya Sangsad*—finally completed and inaugurated in 1982. It was this monumental achievement, along with Islam's Chetana Seminars, that led to the creation of a culture of modern architecture in Bangladesh.

Graduating from the Bangladesh University of Engineering and Technology in 1989, and establishing his own architectural practice in 1995, Azam, like many other young Bengali architects, would be influenced by this regionally inflected modern tradition, as is particularly evident in his Kazedewan Apartments realized in Dhaka in 2002. Among other unique features, this prototypical apartment block makes use of unusually thin cantilevering canopies as shading devices over the main living spaces. At the same time, these same canopies, with occasional pierced openings, constitute a "crowning crescendo" of over-sailing parasols at the top of the building. However, the most surprising aspect of this "structural trope," aside from its thinness, is the bull-nosed profile of its edge, modeled after the equally thin over-sailing roofs of Frank Lloyd Wright's famous Fallingwater, built within the Bear Run Nature Reserve, Pennsylvania, and completed in 1939. This was not, in fact, the only rubric Azam inherited from Wright, the other being Wright's lifelong insistence on the integration of culture and nature. It is a testament to the high level of building culture in Dhaka that the realization of Azam's vision required not only auspicious builders but also talented structural engineers to calculate and position the steel reinforcement of the building's thin cantilevered parasols along with the design of the antiseismic, reinforced concrete frame construction—essential for supporting the heavy weight of the water pools and planting troughs—integrated into the apartments nine floors above grade.

Azam's mid-rise, brick and concrete apartment syntax and, above all, the use of "fair-faced" concrete, was applied by the architect with equal competence to a sequence of large private residences, beginning with the Mizan Residence built in the elite suburb of Gulshan, Dhaka, in 2003, and the more elaborate and extensive Meghna Residence, built in the older, more

Meghna Residence, Dhaka, 2005

prestigious enclave of Dhanmondi, in Dhaka, in 2005. This first sequence of large houses culminated in the extravagant Salauddin Ahmed Residence, realized in Gulshan in 2011, and constructed entirely of fair-faced, reinforced concrete of a quality comparable to that of the Japanese master-architect Tadao Ando. Adhering meticulously to Ando's disciplined approach to casting concrete, Azam paid close attention to all the nuances of his exceptionally demanding method, ranging from the precise mix of sand, cement, and aggregate, to the spacing of the reinforcing bars and restriction of the depth of each lift, to ensure sufficient vibration of the concrete during the casting process. Equally crucial here were the strength and precise fabrication of the formwork in order to resist the expansion of the concrete during the casting process.

As in the "second modernity" of his apartment buildings—to coin Ulrich Beck's felicitous phrase—Azam, in his audacious design of the Ahmed Residence, was evidently influenced by the "first modernity" of the European avant-garde of the early 1920s, specifically by the leading architects of the Dutch Neoplastic movement, Theo Van Doesburg and Gerrit Rietveld. Their abstract, pinwheeling, orthogonal compositions seem to have been the inspiration behind Azam's assembly of three-story, high-ceilinged spaces, which open off the monumental void of the indoor swimming pool that occupies the prominent central area of the ground floor. Although this void, rising for the full height of the house and open to the air, is shaded from the sun by brise soleil, it nonetheless remains exposed to heavy rain during the monsoon season. Although the high-ceilinged, re-entrant spaces opening off the pool are suffused with the gray light of the concrete, this is mediated by the warm light emanating from the timber joinery of the fenestration that separates the main spaces of the house from the central void of the pool.

The undeniably civic scale of the Ahmed house is echoed in Azam's designs for the Ahmed family burial compound, established as a well-maintained, rectangular green earthwork, elevated above the ground and held in place by concrete retaining walls, in the midst of a palm-laden, Edenic landscape. Erected in Botkhil, Noakhali, in 2012, this site is accessed by a monumental staircase rising to the top of the podium and by an equally monumental, reinforced concrete portico opening onto the compound. Furnished with a simple bench, the portico was conceived as a meditation space, looking over the final resting place of the dynastic couple, recalling Carlo Scarpa's arcosolium in the Brion Cemetery in Treviso (1969–1978). At the same time, this earthwork also harked back to the burial mounds of Bengal's prehistoric past, as typified by the Mahasthangarh in Bogra, Bangladesh, dating from the 3rd century BC.

As Bangaldeshi architect and historian Kazi Khaleed Ashraf reminds us, the affluent patronage of the Bengali upper middle class depended, directly or indirectly, on the exponential growth of Bangladesh's textile industry, whose exports today are on par with those of India. As he puts it, the prosperity of this class, "... encouraged by commodity culture and transnational options, is no longer averse to displaying flamboyance." Perhaps as a consequence of this continuing affluence, there is a discernible increase in the sculptural aspect of Azam's architecture, most noticeable in the exuberant plasticity of the Mamun Residence, completed to Azam's designs in the port city of Chittagong, south of Dhaka, in 2013. Structured around a rectangular open-air swimming pool, this work may be seen as the converse of the Ahmed Residence,

Mamun Residence, Chittagong, 2008
SA Family Graveyard, Noakhali, 2012

in as much as the cubic volumes of the house are distributed horizontally around the pool as a composition of freestanding walls, cut-away planes, and deep, cantilevered, flat roofs. In many ways, this work is a tour de force, combining the perfection of fair-faced concrete à la Ando with a cubistic planar display, reminiscent of Wright.

Surely one of the most atypical developments of Azam's early career is the S P Setia curtain-walled corporate office building, erected as a lone monolith in the midst of a 5,000-acre, unspoiled meadowland site in "Setia Alam," located in Shah Alam City, Malaysia, close to Kuala Lumpur. Realized over the years 2012–2014, this work involved the invention of the extra tall, reinforced concrete column which, like Le Corbusier's infamous piloti, supported the seven-story office building and its over-sailing parasol roof. An excessively tall version of the same column is repeated in a twelve-column peristyle, dramatically rising at one end of the office block to support the overrun of the parasol. These columns, like others beneath the block itself, rise out of a rainwater-harvesting sump that extends into the landscape; a feature which, from a certain angle, provides the illusion that the building is floating. In addition to these formal nuances, the entire building is double-glazed in low-E glass to reduce both heat gain and cooling load in high summer, a provision that enabled the building to earn a premium rating as a sustainable structure.

SP Setia, Malaysia, 2014

However, the most dramatic formal trope to emerge out of this development was undoubtedly the extra tall column, which will play such a prominent role in Azam's Bangladesh Chancery Complex in Islamabad, Pakistan, designed in 2015 and now scheduled for completion in 2025. Although the tall column is the primary plastic element of the peristyle supporting the monumental parasol of the chancery, its heterotopic application—with some colonnades rising out of water, and others firmly grounded in the podium, and single columns arranged in a ring to support the perimeter of a circular aperture above—is sufficient to deprive the freestanding column of its former classical association. There is also one instance of a column cantilevering down from the soffit of the concrete slab above, as an ironic parody in concrete of the typically broken stone column invariably found in classical sites. Beneath all of this, the earthwork, together with the office and residential accommodation integrated into its form, is faced throughout in brickwork, as are the retaining walls integrating the chancery into the site. The full significance of this work has been made abundantly clear by Azam in the following explicatory text:

"Bangladesh, with its three thousand years of Bengal civilization, and Pakistan, with its history of five thousand years of Indus Valley civilization, share a common journey through the past. The resemblance between these two countries lies in their historic ruins, particularly in the terracotta brick sites that share a common ground in their design. This inspired me to conceive of the site as an 'archeological landscape,' a meeting place for two civilizations. Another key role in this design is the delta of Bangladesh, the largest on earth, bringing water in abundance to the alluvial plains, and Pakistan's contoured landscape, with its mountain ranges around Islamabad. So the concept for this project evolved from a single horizontal line representing the land of Bangladesh, against the vertically majestic Margalla Hills of Islamabad, and a subtle intervention into nature, with a large water body representing the delta, collected from rainfall. The flat rectilinear parasol *jali* (roof) echoes the gentle landscapes of Bangladesh, complementing the regal Margalla Hills."

The forthcoming realization of the Bangladesh Chancery will testify not only to the prestigious standing of the architect but also to the wealth and confidence of Bangladesh, as this work will represent to the world at large both the continued peaceful coexistence of the two Islamic states within the Subcontinent, and the historical role played by India, half a century ago, in intervening and ending the devastating conflict between them.

This magnanimous and monumental work paradoxically brings the sculpturally exuberant phase of Azam's career to a close, as his Shatotto studio shifts its emphasis to the social welfare aspects of its production. Although he has continued to design luxury houses for the elite—as in the Asif Zahir Residence first designed for the prestigious Gulshan district of Dhaka in 2017—he has done so only as if it were a modular, repeatable bourgeois prototype, wherein a cubistic, orthogonal reinforced concrete frame can be articulated to provide the necessary prerequisites, such as exceptionally generous living spaces along with other luxury features like hanging gardens, ornamental pools, and built-in gymnasia.

As a result, there follows, as intrinsic to his Shatotto "green-living" agenda, the studio's radical restoration of existing public recreational spaces within the densely built-up fabric of Dhaka. These include the Bahadur Shah Park, the Delowar Hossain Area Development, the Osmani Udyan, and Rasulbagh Shishu Park in the Azimpur district of the city. In almost every instance, the task has involved the radical reparation of the ground surface. This green agenda has also attempted to introduce a new urban scale into Dhaka, as in its proposal for the Aga Khan Academy conceived as a perimeter development around a large square green space in the middle of existing fabric. This work, like the Junior School with which it is associated, has returned Azam to reinforced concrete, brick-faced construction as a normative Bangladeshi building technique and aesthetic, pioneered by Muzharul Islam in collaboration with the American architect Stanley Tigerman in the mid 1960s. The Shatotto studio slogan, "architecture for green living," testifies to Azam's heightened awareness of the challenges posed to the poorer countries of the Global South by escalating climate change and by the constant onslaught of the worldwide neoliberal economy, whose effects have been particularly pernicious in the extreme monsoon climate of the Bengal Delta, where, after the rainy season, two thirds of the country is under water.

Among the socially committed works that Shatotto has achieved in recent years, two park restorations in Dhaka, the Rasulbagh Shishu Park, and the Delowar Hossain Area Development stand out for their social relevance and for their ecological, low-maintenance character. Moreover, the extensive perimeter planting in both parks contributes to Dhaka's current policy of increasing the density of shade trees throughout the city. While they are both exemplary restorations, the Rasulbagh Shishu Park (2018–2021) is the larger and more elaborately equipped of the two, featuring a three-story service building with an open-air cafeteria on its roof, partially covered by a shade canopy. A singular new flood-control feature known as the aqua trench system has also been installed in order to maintain the separation of storm and sewage water during the rainy season. In addition to the cafeteria, the service building provides a women's club, storage, restrooms, and importantly, a plant for filtering rainwater so as to render it potable, while on the first and second floors respectively, there is a children's library and a councilor's room, plus a gymnasium above.

Central to the reallocation of space within the existing park is the provision of a playground for young children and a promenade for adults to stroll along in the evening. Flood lighting is provided so that the sports facility may be used after dark. The latter is divided into two 20-meter-wide play areas, separated by a 2-meter-high wire-mesh metal fence. The perimeter of the park is furnished with low sitting benches built out of brick. Both parks use mainly the same species of plants, plus, as far as possible, locally sourced materials including reinforced concrete slabs and concrete work cast on site, brick paving, and perforated terracotta blockwork for the *jali* where required. The smaller Delowar Hossain Area Development has only one fenced sports field, plus a shallow pond for young children to cool off during the heat of high summer.

One of the most important realizations of the Shatotto studio to date is the Mayor Mohammad Hanif Jame Mosque, completed in Dhaka in 2018, whose largely reinforced concrete construction is clad in brick inside and out. The complex is comprised of the two-story mosque itself, with its superimposed prayer halls, plus a two-story communal block situated on either side of a slightly elevated paved forecourt, and linked by a "dematerialized" glazed pedestrian bridge at the first floor. The most striking aspect of the entire complex is its monumental brick mass, which backs onto the pre-existing mosque, while of the greatest poetic character is the colossal concrete entry portico and stepped entrance, leading onto the central paved plaza, or *shaan*. The superimposed prayer halls are each structured around eight reinforced concrete mushroom columns, and feature a top-lit slot of space, at the base of which is a channel of purifying water, directly accessible from the lower hall. The whole complex has something of a labyrinthine character, providing small-scale sacred spaces throughout, intermixed with more secular functions. Perhaps the most amenable aspect of the whole project is the way in which it presents itself as a community center for the entire neighborhood.

After a distinguished career as a Bengali architect of exceptional talent, technological ingenuity, and sophisticated imagination, culminating in a brilliant monumental representation of the diplomatic prowess of the nation state, Rafiq Azam has now emerged, through his Shatotto practice, as a socio-ecologically committed architect, profoundly involved with the welfare of society as a whole.

Delowar Hossain Area Development, Lalbagh, Dhaka, 2024

unfolding nothingness

SA RESIDENCE

Gulshan, Dhaka
2005–2011

Water, the most precious and abundant element in Bangladesh, is our lifeblood and provides for this country's poetic essence. Set within the largest delta on Earth, Bangladesh has around 1,200 intricate water channels originating in the Himalayas that lead into the Bay of Bengal. During the monsoon, these rivers inundate two-thirds of the country's landmass and literally define its central landscape. When the waters recede, they leave fine layers of fertile alluvial soil and entire regions are transformed into large patchworks of paddy fields that dance along with the winds.

As the Bengali philosopher and Sufi mystic Lalon (1774–1890) described: "If there is not one thing inside the body, then it is not outside the body either." Just as each human being has two elements—their body as a shell and their mind as the soul—architecture similarly has the built structure as its shell and the natural environment as its soul. Both the shell and the soul are clearly distinct and yet entirely interdependent.

In this private family residence, the spaces are inspired by both urban and rural typologies. The courtyard connected to the adjacent pond, visible in many traditional buildings, was designed to adapt to its urban context, with articulations on the south and southeast corners to welcome the summer breeze and the winter sun. The light inside caresses the walls, just as the waters outside embrace this land. One's whole being is invited to meld into this tranquil setting to escape the surrounding city.

page 22
Ground level
meets the water.

previous page
Tranquil light
on third level.

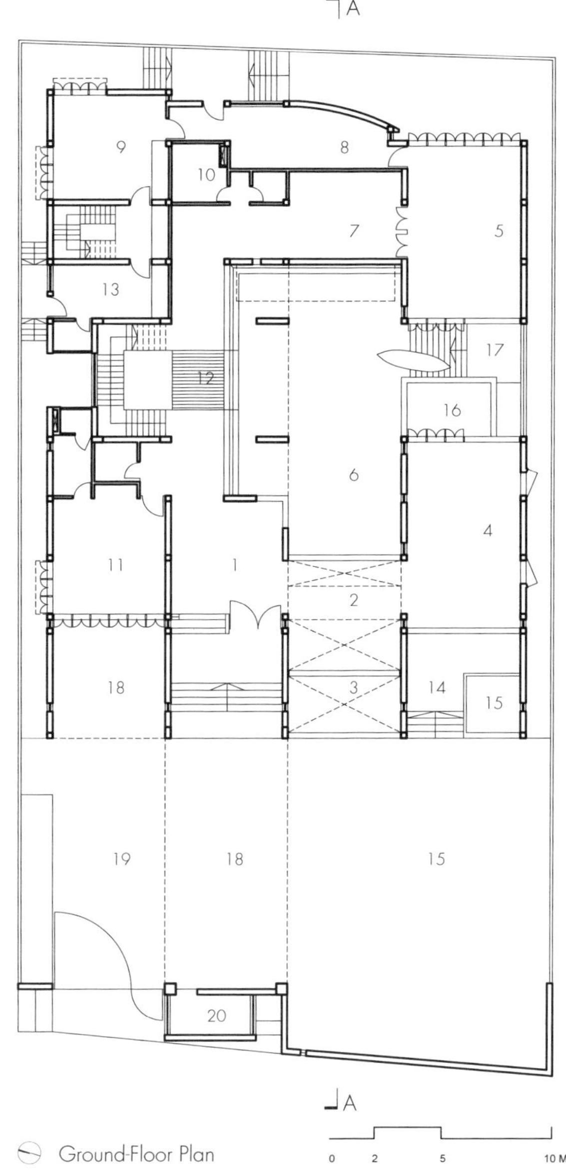

Ground-Floor Plan

1. lobby
2. lounge
3. water body
4. living room
5. dining room
6. swimming pond
7. deck
8. pantry
9. kitchen
10. sauna
11. guest room
12. wooden bridge
13. driver's room
14. veranda
15. garden
16. greenery
17. ghat
18. parking
19. driveway
20. security entrance

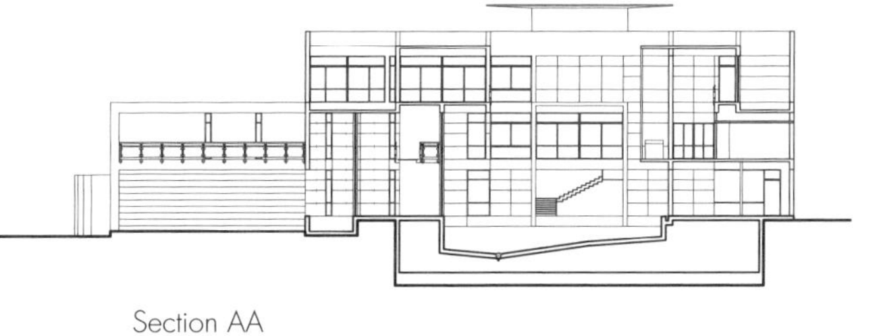
Section AA

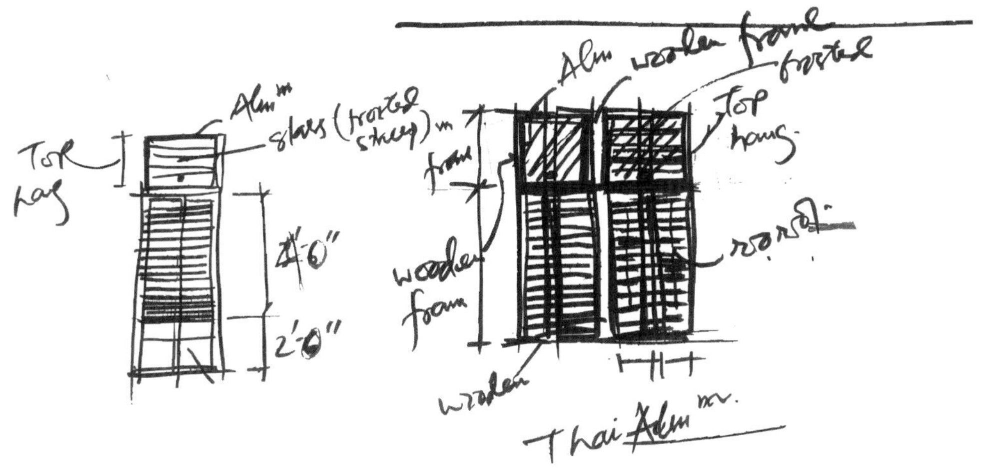

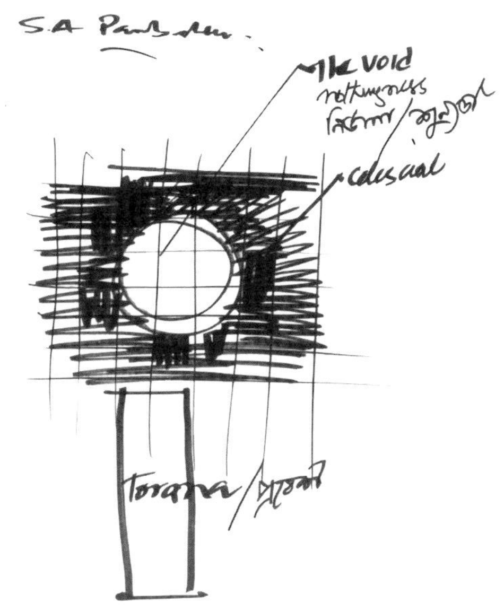

A small dinghy boat waiting by the ghat,
a patch of green, light and silence.
Space becomes our natural habitat,
unfolding nothingness.

Rafiq Azam

When light returns
to its source, it takes nothing
back from the illuminated.

Rumi

SHAPING DHAKA
SHAMSUL WARES

nature and architecture

Since Bangladesh's independence in 1971, its capital city Dhaka has undergone overwhelming demographic growth due mainly to economic migration from rural areas. Over the last fifty years, this city's population has increased exponentially, from about 2 million in 1974 to over 24 million in 2024. Comparatively speaking, in this same time frame, New York's population has grown by around 2 million, from 18 to 20 million, and yet its metropolitan area (circa 34,490 km^2) is more than 20 times that of Dhaka city (circa 1,530 km^2). Under such contrasting circumstances, Dhaka, home to over 4 million slum dwellers, has been experiencing unprecedented over-exploitation of its land and water resources, ever-diminishing open spaces, inadequate power supplies, poorly managed sanitation facilities, indiscriminate demolition of historical edifices, relentless traffic congestion, and above all, poverty and homelessness. All this has turned Dhaka into a troubled city, where the practice of architecture has become a far more challenging job. Mega projects have typically been undertaken by government authorities without sufficient concern or research into the socioeconomic and historical contexts and consequences. Tall buildings are mushrooming across its skyline, much like in other fast-growing cities in Asia and the Middle East, without expertly handled urban planning and clear environmental understanding and decision-making. Despite such extreme contradictions and anomalies, surprisingly Dhaka has emerged as the fourth-largest megacity in the world, after Tokyo, Delhi, and Shanghai, according to the 2025 World Population Review.

Contemporary architecture has ever more intricate relationships with art and culture, urban growth, and both local and national narratives, which are all by their nature constantly evolving. As such, designing a new building or city space, as an authentic catalyst of metropolitan life, is necessarily more complex here. Territorial organization and planning for more equitable provisions and access to housing, community facilities, public spaces, transport networks, and other services and infrastructures are increasingly problematic. This clearly poses new questions for architects here and within this entire region. Design professionals must rethink their roles and their potential impact and influence on society. Refering to Tadao Ando's work, architect Masao Furuyama asserts that architecture's ideal is to form a spatial model of the world and its ultimate ambition is to "awaken man's sensibilities."[1] Architecture must certainly solve more problems and provide order, but also contribute to social meaning and collective values. Its dynamism and aesthetics, even through contrasting forms and space, need to generate emotive power and direct relevance.

Since his very first built project, Rafiq Azam has consistently aimed to formulate a unique model of architecture for Bangladesh, not only due to this country's specific tropical climate but also in close relationship to its cultural traditions and realities. At the same time, his work endeavors to instill a sense of calm and comfort, evoking emotional responses and developing our awareness of the natural elements that surround us. His main objective has always been to shape a new and contextual

approach to modern design that addresses the ever-changing social demands of a post-Independence Bangladesh. For him, this new architecture must also embrace new technologies and construction standards. Besides creating beautiful internal spaces, his buildings express exterior interests and personalities that reflect those of the city itself.

Over three decades, Azam has confidently established his own studious vernacular. For both private and public spaces, his signature fair-faced concrete, exposed brick walls, generous terraces, projected eaves, parasol roofs, and clear glazing are all carefully curated alongside his use of vegetation, water bodies, natural light, and airflow, which have become the true protagonists on his spatial stage. Even the smallest natural elements have their poetic roles in his creative process of "generating energy" through the built form, and not only as mechanisms for saving resources or environmental consciousness. Vegetation is often coupled with water bodies in elegant interpretations of the sun and the monsoon within the overall deltaic landscape of this country. Today he is recognized as one of the most accomplished architects in twenty-first-century Bangladesh and his work is ubiquitous in every corner of both old and new Dhaka, as well as in several prestigious international projects for which he has gained well-deserved acclaim for his contributions to global design culture.

Born in 1963, Azam's maternal grandmother's house in Urdu Road was just a stone's throw from the family home in Lalbagh, in the old city of Dhaka. This area is renowned for its pink stone Lalbagh Fort, built in 1678 by Mughal Prince Muhammad Azam Shah, the son of Emperor Aurangzeb, who became the future emperor, within a walled complex that accommodates the governor's residence and the tomb of Pari Bibi, the emperor's much-loved daughter, with a mosque and Mughal garden. Spacious lawns, fountains, and water channels frame its central grounds. Situated on the banks of the Buriganga River, south of the city, its huge, arched entrance was also the gateway for Rafiq Azam's childhood inspirations.

Azam began his schooling at Nabakumar Institute (est.1916) and later attended West End High School (est.1920). In those days, schools in Old Dhaka taught "morality," with a strong emphasis on academic achievement and earning a simple, honest, community-based living. These were broadly considered middle-class values and teachers often modeled these ideals themselves. At the tender age of seven, Rafiq demonstrated a keen interest in and aptitude for painting, being quite subconsciously attracted to beauty and finding meaning in its myriad forms. In 1975, in the seventh grade, he began taking lessons from Abu Tahir Babu, a student of Fine Arts at Dhaka University, who taught him the basics of watercolor painting. Through careful guidance, Rafiq was captivated by its translucent unpredictabilities and the magical qualities of water and colors combined. He soon began winning awards and prizes in both national and regional student painting competitions, including the

Lalbagh Fort in Old Dhaka, 2024

Its construction was begun in 1678 by Prince Azam Shah, son of the Emporer Aurangzeb, during his time as the Viceroy of Bengal. Image courtesy of Pinu Rahman

The Boat, watercolor by Rafiq Azam, 1975

At thirteen years of age, he received the Jawaharlal Nehru Memorial Gold Medal for this painting.

Azam Residence, Lalbagh, Old Dhaka

1976 Jawharlal Nehru Memorial Gold Medal from Shankar's International Children's Competitions (SICC) in Delhi at thirteen years of age. He later graduated from Kabi Nazrul Government College in Lakshmibazar, Old Dhaka, and by this time had also developed a fascination for design. Architecture eventually became his ideal combination of art, science, and technology interests. In 1989, he graduated as an architect from Bangladesh University of Engineering and Technology (BUET) and his career began to gain momentum.

Rafiq's father, Mohammad Azam, was a businessman and his mother, Anguri Begum Azam, raised their five sons and four daughters, with Rafiq sixth in line. The family lived in a modest single-story house in Atash Khana Lane in Lalbagh, which was divided into three blocks that were built in different periods: the front facing the laneway housed the living room, two study areas, three bedrooms, and a linear southward veranda. The rear section consisted of one bedroom and bathroom, and the middle section consisted of the family dining room, kitchen, and storerooms, with a detached toilet and tap water facility. The open courtyard between the front and middle blocks, protecting them from the noisy, dusty streets, quite naturally became the "soul" of their house. Full of sunlight, rain, and breathing space, it was Rafiq's mother's favorite place in the world.

After his father's death in 1984, his widowed mother entrusted him with the responsibility of designing their new house on their land in Lalbagh after demolishing the old house. At the time, Azam was only a second-year architecture student at BUET, but he enthusiastically accepted the challenge. His father had previously appointed an architect for their new house in 1981, but due to financial constraints, only part of the building was completed according to its original design. Instead of demolishing this partial construction, Azam incorporated it into his new plans to reduce the extra costs. He was well aware of his mother's emotional attachment to their old courtyard and her preference for living on the ground floor, where she could touch the soil and tend her garden. With this in mind, he diligently developed a design that recreated a ground-floor courtyard with the proximity of nature. Eventually, he developed a geometrically asymmetrical open plan with a simple pathway connecting the living, dining, and family spaces while incorporating separate bedrooms and open terraces with pergolas, plants, and sunshine.

Upon its completion (1988), their two-story Azam Residence not only delighted Rafiq's mother but also became a model of contemporary living for the locals. With its unpretentious simplicity and order within closed, semi-closed, and open sky spaces, their family home stands as one of his most remarkable achievements. Louis Kahn often spoke of his Trenton Bath House (1955–1959) as a turning point in his design philosophy: "From this project came a generative force which is recognizable in every building I have done since."[2] Essentially, the design principles applied in the Azam Residence, his first completed project at twenty-five years of age, formulated the DNA of his entire body of work. These ideas have reoccurred consistently with various additions, shifts in focus, and much greater sophistication in all of Rafiq's later works, shaping Dhaka's architectural backdrop.

Soon after graduating in 1989, Azam established an architectural practice with three of his classmates, but later opened his independent studio in 1995 called Shatotto—architecture for green living. In 2001, he was commissioned to design a building in Old Dhaka for multifamily accommodation. The site was small, only 267.66 m^2 on Noor Fateh Lane in Khajedewan, and the client, who was also the landowner, wanted to construct three apartments on each floor to rent out to lower-middle-class families. He expected his architect to go ahead with a free hand over everything. Although the dimensions were very tight, Azam saw this as his opportunity to realize his vision of developing a climatically responsive and culturally vibrant urban fabric for the old town. His ability to weave together open spaces with closed rooms through a "circulatory system" of natural light and air deep within the structure, which he had experimented with within his Lalbagh family home, was further elaborated and intensified for this multistory Khajedewan Apartments project (2001–2002).

Dipu Sharmin Residence, Dhaka

Azam designed for a total of fourteen families over five stories, with three on each floor. Space for one unit at the ground level adjacent to the access road was left open for a spacious entryway and social activities. Three two-bedroom apartments on each floor, approximately 68 m^2 each, were cleverly grouped into split levels around a dog-legged staircase that ends at the roof line. Despite such tight parameters, Azam still managed to provide each apartment with a feeling of spaciousness, utilizing ample light and airflow. Although the building is basically rectangular in form, he divided the surfaces with verandas, cavities, recesses, and gaps between apartments, introducing light wells, terraces, and vegetation spaces to facilitate air currents and allow natural light to penetrate deep inside the built forms. Instead of creating a solid cuboid structure, he used horizontal and vertical perforations to scale down the masses. A curious feature of this design is the top floor, where Azam created an open space and reduced the built form by judiciously terminating the building with a thin concrete parasol roof. The shaded void afforded underneath the roof makes the building more inviting and aesthetically engaging. But the most compelling outcome is that most of the tenants enjoy the building so much that they want to live there for the rest of their lives. Many had previously endured rooms without windows in this same neighborhood. Indeed, these Khajedewan Apartments remain one of Rafiq Azam's most rewarding local achievements.

In his six-story Gulfeshan Apartments (2000–2002), designed for twenty families in the more affluent area of new Dhaka, beside Gulshan Lake, Azam split the built forms into two masses to create a raised garden in between, keeping the existing mature trees on site. This lush garden courtyard with paving and sitting areas provides a tranquil ambiance alongside the lake. The plan-forms of these two buildings are derived from the very same principles he used for the Khazedewan Apartments project, with subtle variations. The exterior of these buildings is adorned with vertical, tapered brick masses and intermittent brick gaps that allude to local archaeology, reminding us that "New Dhaka" is a natural extension and an evolution of the old city.

The four-story Meghna Residence (2003–2005) in Dhanmondi, Dhaka, is one of the very large single-family homes designed by Azam for an industrialist owner. The character of the planning and built form of this lavish house resembles that of his Khazedewan and Gulfeshan projects. Here, a U-shaped planform is developed around a private court at the ground-floor level facing south-west to allow ample air and light to flow into the building. Fair-faced concrete and exposed brick walls used in conjunction with large glass surfaces and meticulous detailing juxtapose its solidity and transparency. This house is adorned with plentiful vegetation to accomplish an explicit sense of "tropical architecture." Its rectangular rooftop swimming pool with shading and garden trims provides a feeling of contemporary openness and freedom but also echoes the age-old deltaic landscape of Bangladesh. From this project onward, water, vegetation, and sunlight became Azam's most fundamental elements in his interpretation of Bangladeshi architecture.

His much-acclaimed SA Residence, a three-story single-family home in Gulshan (2005–2011), consists of architectural concrete combined with an elegant wood frame and clear glazing. While Louis Kahn's National Assembly Building, finally completed in 1982 for the newly independent Bangladesh, is surrounded by a vast water body separating it from the capital's busy roads, Azam's contrasting design for this home enclosed a central water body at the ground level with a lofty glazed canopy roof. This beautifully introverted, sculptural concept is carefully proportioned with proceeding and receding concrete forms that are somewhat reminiscent of the De Stijl movement in early twentieth-century Dutch art. The warm timber glow of its glazing frames against the stoically pared-down concrete surfaces, and establishes a quiet equilibrium within and throughout the house. The lush garden terrace, adorned with concrete ribbed pergolas on the first floor above the entry portico, recalls the one Azam first conceived for his mother's house in Lalbagh.

By 2018, Shatotto's "green living" dictum was clearly on display in the three-story Dipu Sharmin House (2013–2016) in Nikunja, Dhaka. Being a small site with a height restriction of 13 meters, a basement floor was introduced to accommodate various functional requirements and to articulate cleverly compact living spaces with several lofts, natural light wells, and a remarkable arrangement of water bodies. As the building climbs upward, lush vegetation dominates at different levels and practically turns the whole house into a kind of botanical architecture. By reducing the imposition of built-forms, Azam has meticulously curated an untameable garden, as if to invite a tropical jungle to take over the landscape. This overwhelmingly naturalistic approach has erased any tension between the man-made form and the space, two essential elements of architecture, and allowed for the silent drama of nature to take the stage.

Over the last two decades, a consumerist society has evolved in Bangladesh due to the steady industrialization of its emerging economy. As a result, a new demand for high-end residential architecture with modern comforts for exclusive lifestyles has grown. Property developers in this country have been pressuring architects to the limits of their knowledge and creativity to make living spaces pleasurable and attractive to potential buyers. Expectations for quality materials, innovative design concepts, and sustainable solutions are high, with customers wanting personalized, sophisticated, and exceptional design experiences. Under these circumstances, Azam's multistory apartment design has adapted to a more formal, monumental, urbanistic style that is in some ways more impersonal. Although consistently adhering to his own original principles, his attention has necessarily shifted from the intimate scale of his early projects to the grander civic scale, with architectonic innovation and a relentless commitment to excellence.

Haque's South Leaf in Gulshan (2017–2021) is a luxurious fourteen-story multifamily building containing twenty-one simplex and two duplex apartments, as well as two basement floors with thirty-six parking spaces. This design, with a largely open ground floor, includes a loft for residential activities as well as lawns, pavements, water bodies, and vegetation to create an opulent vista. The complex has been rendered with clean lines, open spaces, free, robust circular columns, sculptural concrete walls with circular perforations, and obliquely angled suspended concrete walls. Here, form and space compete for attention, with each perfectly balanced.

In recent years, Rafiq Azam has bravely focused his energies on a number of major revitalization projects, in consultation with government agencies, to rejuvenate neglected urban areas and to modernize forgotten parts of Old Dhaka. Projects such as Bahadur Shah Park, Delowar Hossain Area Development, Rasulbagh Shishu Park, and Osmani Udyan are very important initiatives to mend the wounds of the old city and transform slum-like conditions into beautiful parks, sporting grounds, gardens, pavements, seating areas, drinking fountains, and water bodies. By facilitating community enjoyment and harmony, his interventions restore the sense of a shared "neighborhood oasis" in otherwise unsanitary and highly congested streets. Magically brought back to life, these areas now welcome back children and elderly people who were long-deprived of breathing space. But all this has been extremely difficult. Azam has personally endured many struggles, spending huge amounts of time and energy with few financial benefits, to convince government authorities of the advantages of these renewal projects. His reshaping of Dhaka is undertaken with missionary zeal—out of his passion for innovative design and his love for the old city where he was born and raised.

1. Masao Furuyama and Peter Gossel (ed.), *Ando: The Geometry of Human Space*, Architecture Series (Taschen America, 2006).

2. David B. Brownlee and David G. De Long, *Louis I. Kahn: In the Realm of Architecture* (Rizzoli, 1991).

neo-archaic

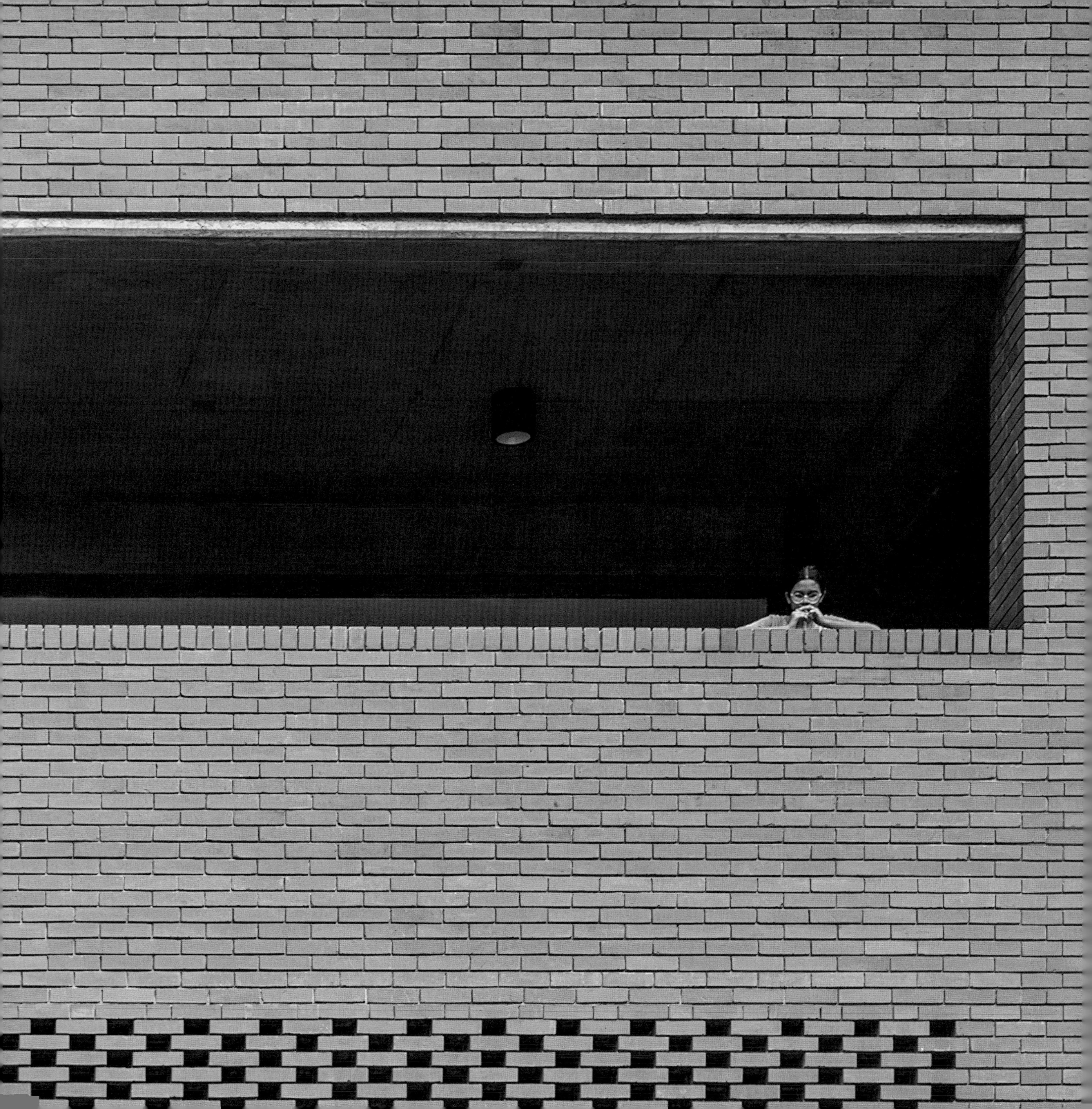

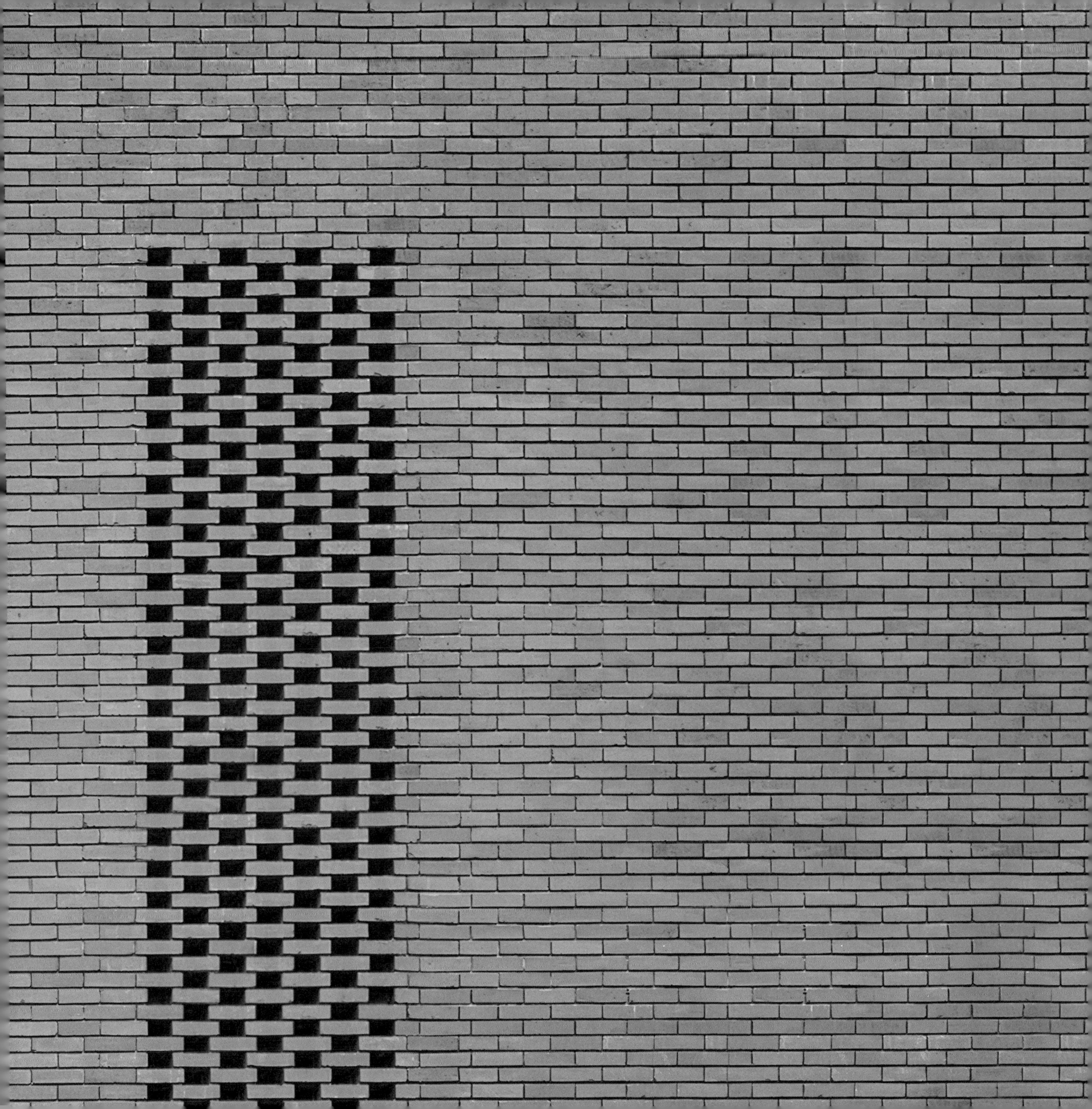

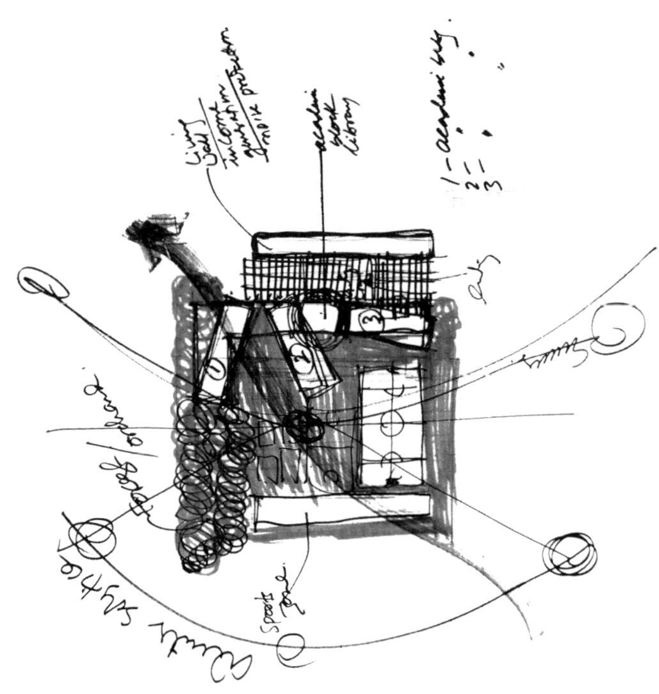

AGA KHAN ACADEMY

Bashundhara, Dhaka

Phase 1 2017–2022

This project was inspired by the "Great Monastery" Somapura Mahavihara (also known as Paharpur Buddhist Vihara), an ancient Buddhist monastic complex located in the Naogaon District of Bangladesh. Constructed in the late 8th century CE by the Pala King Dharmapala, for centuries it served as a renowned intellectual center. It is a UNESCO World Heritage Site and considered one of the largest and most important monasteries in South Asia. With its simple, harmonious lines and profusion of intricately carved decorations, this complex is a powerful architectural paradigm.

The design for the Aga Khan Academy Dhaka received the award for best "Future Education" project at the 2017 World Architecture Festival in Berlin. For this project, the courtyards and spatial organization reflect the languages of Bengali architecture and brick composition, and align with the tropical climate to allow the summer winds and winter sun to enter. Tapping into local craftsmanship, the passageways are supported by brick-clad columns and traditional *jali* (perforated or latticed screens). The large *maidan* (square) is the genius loci at the academy's center, with peripheral courtyards as thresholds to the indoor spaces for age-specific programs. The senior courtyard is designed to sit under planted trees, which inspires group activities. The assembly court, adjacent to the academic block, is intentionally kept devoid of any elements except four trees. According to local legend, the city derived its name from these Dhaak trees, known as "flames of the forest," a species native to the tropical and subtropical regions of the Subcontinent and Southeast Asia. The amphitheater accommodates large gatherings and contains a sandpit that holds water during heavy rains, allowing the children to celebrate nature.

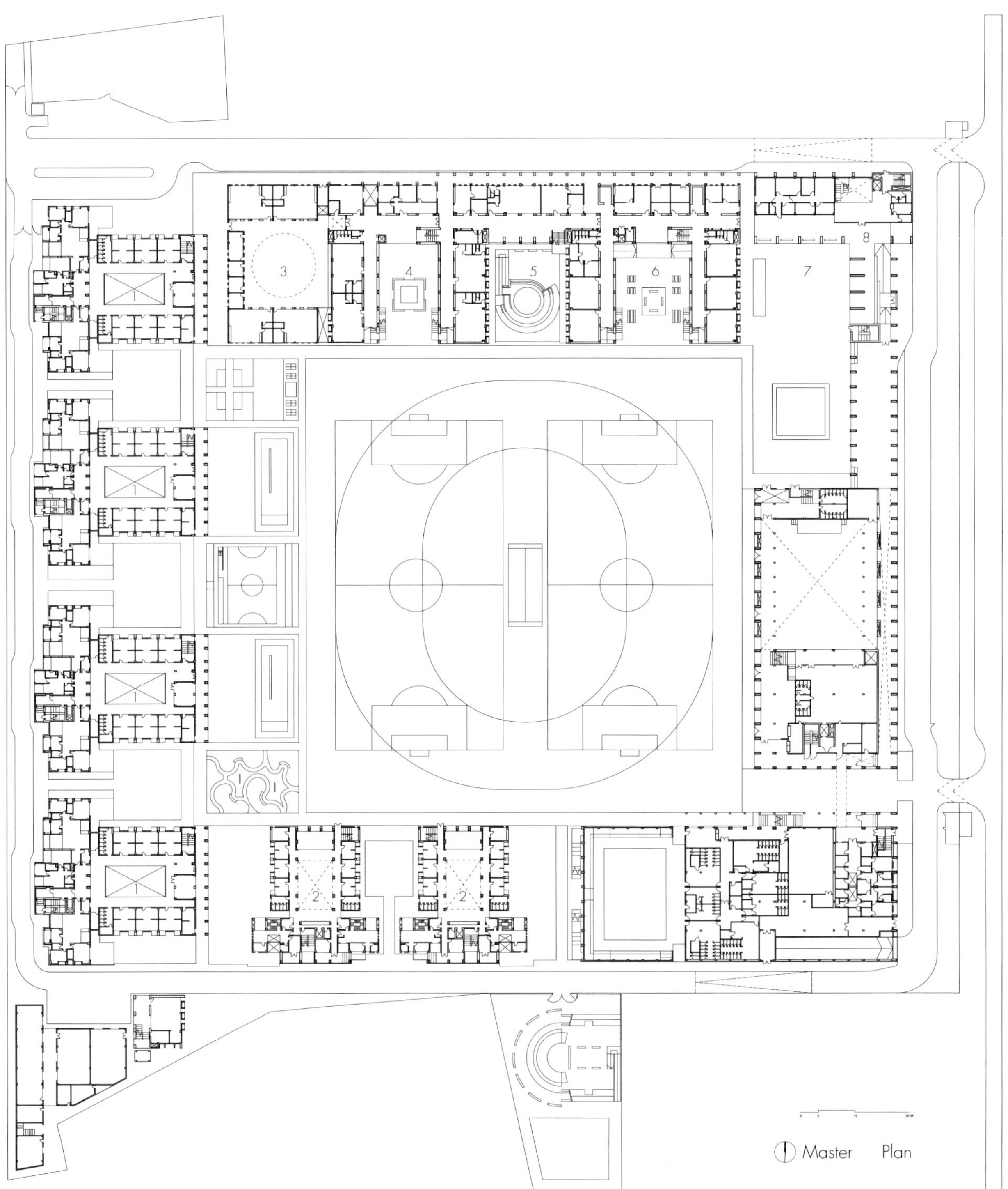

1. middle school residence
2. diploma school residence
3. nursery school courtyard
4. junior courtyard
5. central courtyard
6. senior courtyard
7. assembly courtyard
8. academic building

next page
Clay model of Aga Khan Academy.

INTELLECTUAL
MORAL
PHYSICAL
SPIRITUAL

South-facing courtyard of academic building in the winter.

next page
Niche seating for students.

following pages
Morning light in the senior courtyard.

Maidan (square) view from the south.

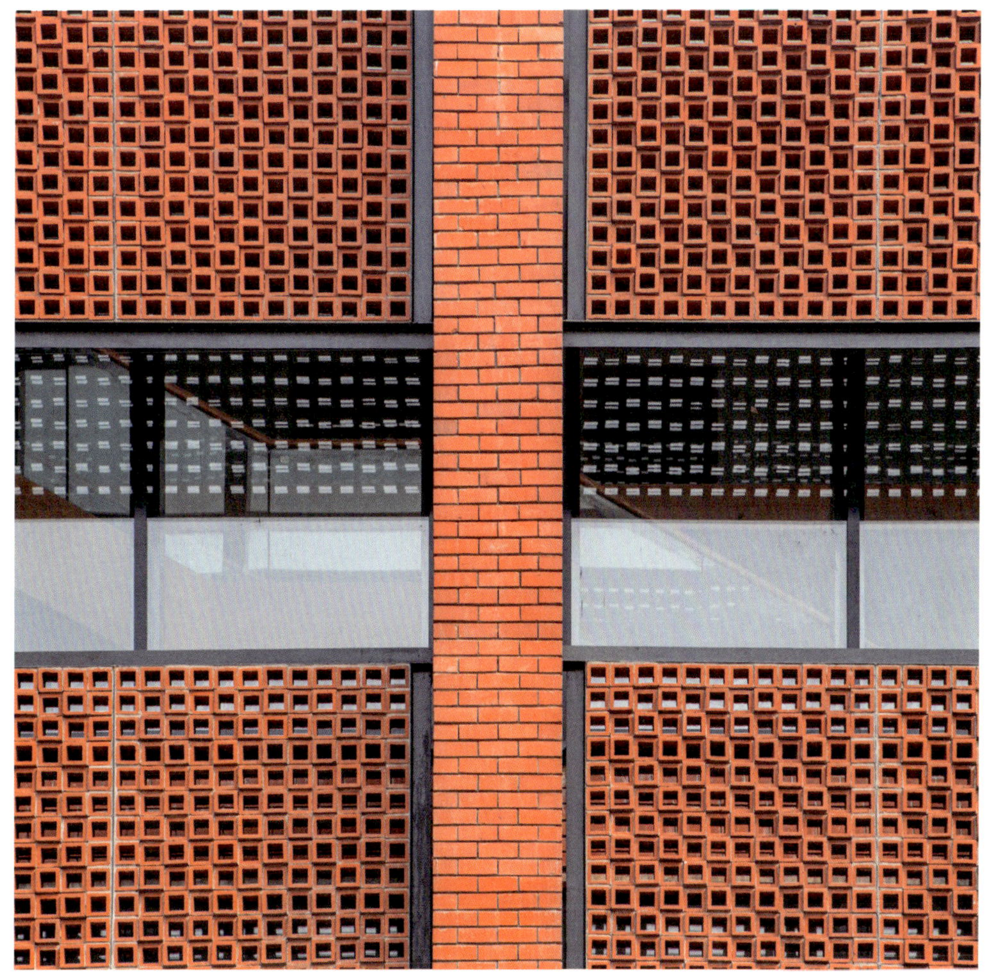

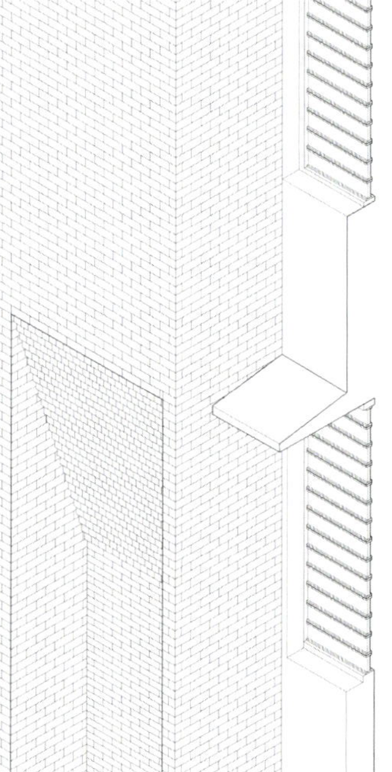

Science laboratory in senior building.

previous page
Dhak trees *(Butea monosperma)* in the assembly court.

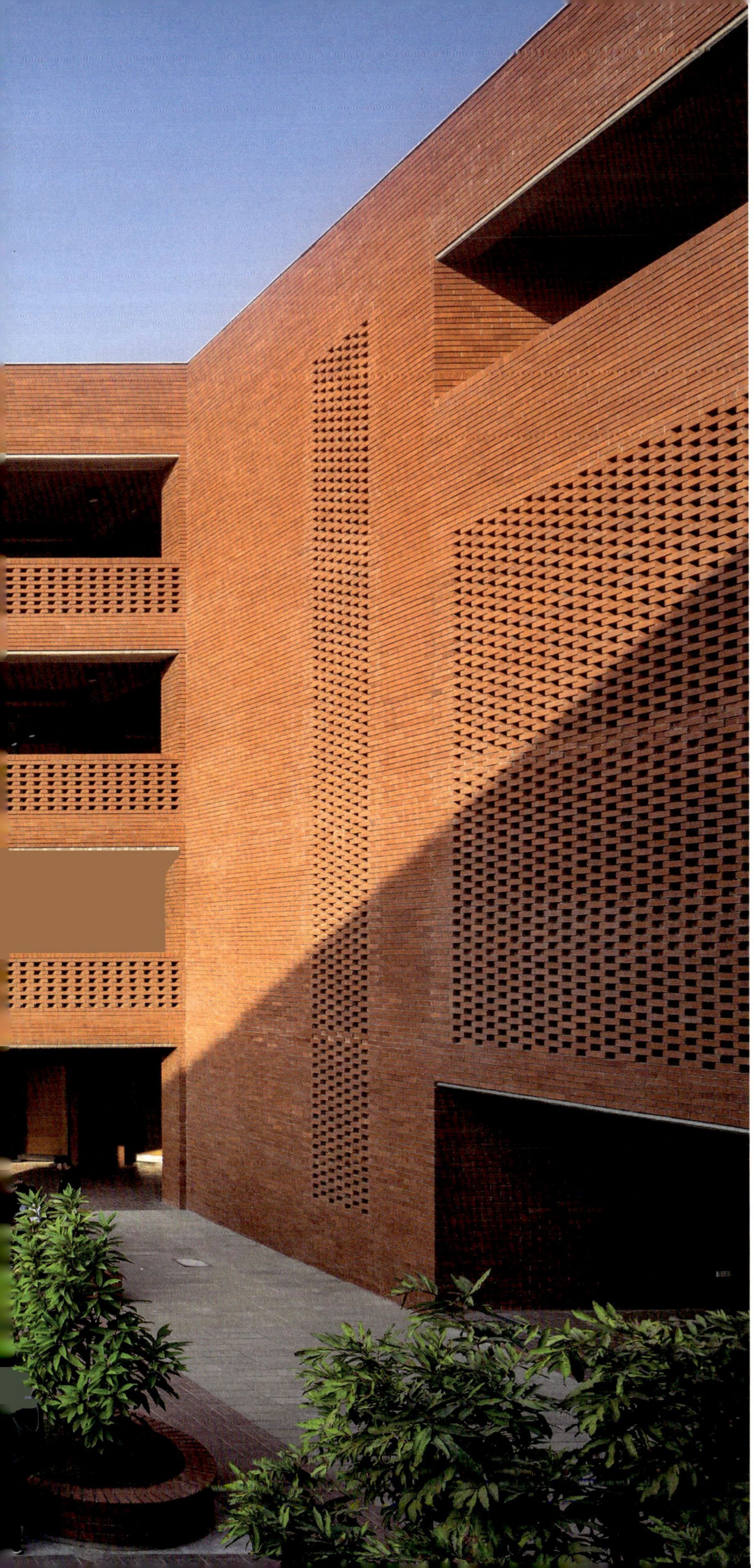

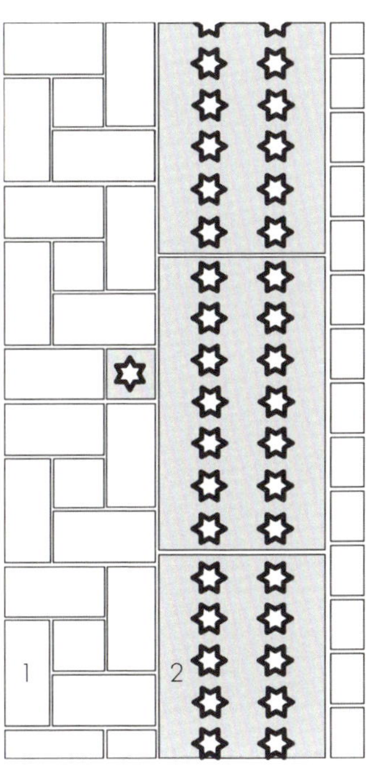

1. clay brick paving
(200 mm x 100 mm x 50 mm).
2. star-shaped openings for drainage
system, in cast iron to prevent rust.

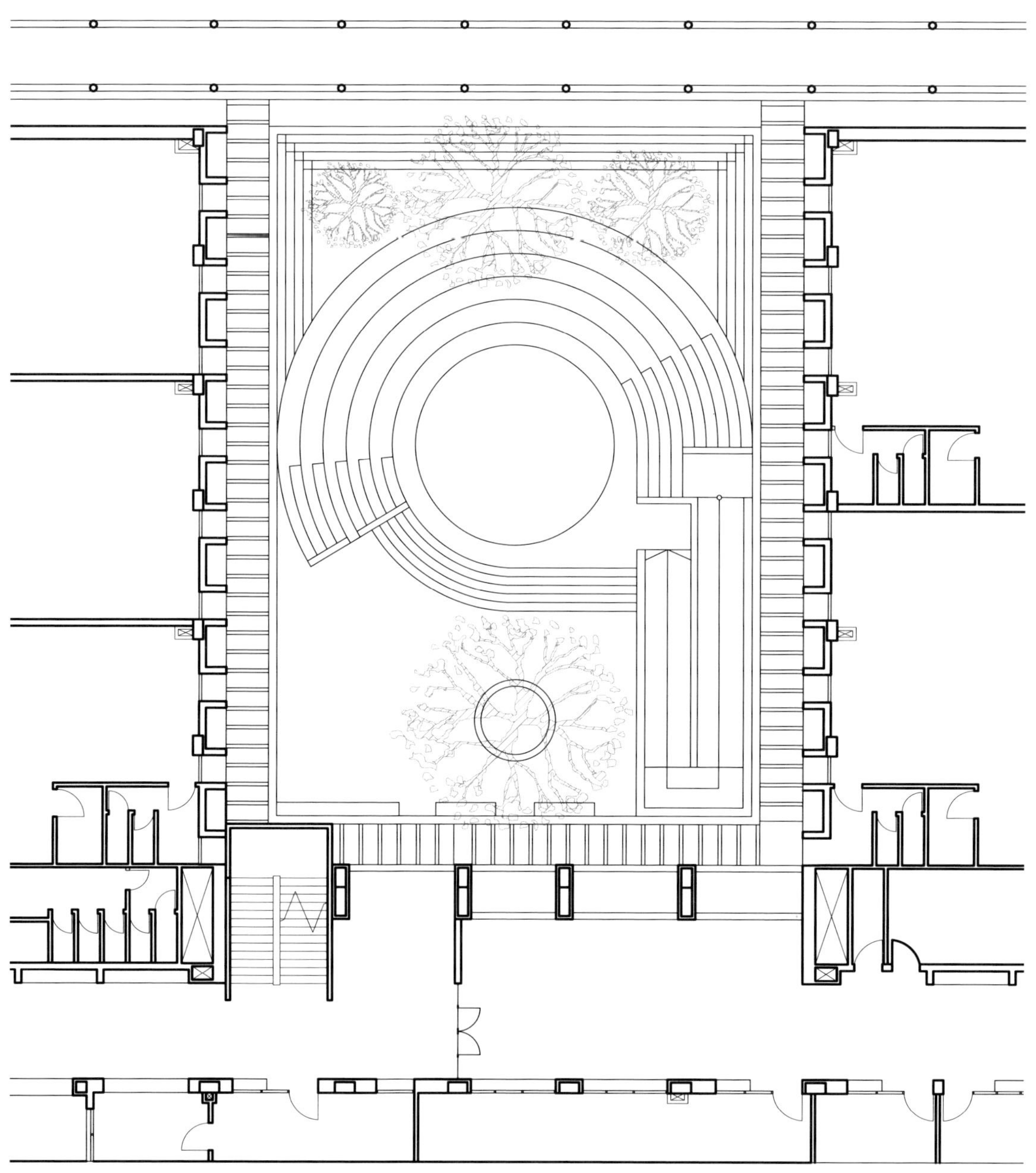

A central courtyard, celebrating the ephemeral beauty of the rainwater in the sandpit.

INSPIRATION WITHIN
FUAD H. MALLICK

memory and style

Modern architecture in Bangladesh began in the 1950s with the pioneering works of architect, urban planner, educator, and activist Muzharul Islam (1923, Murshidabad, British India – 2012, Dhaka, Bangladesh). In 1965, an article in *Architectural Review* (1965) by Otto H. Königsberger proclaimed that Muzharul Islam's works in Bangladesh are of global stature, establishing the systems and principles of modern tropical architecture. Two decades after Independence from British colonial rule of the Indian subcontinent and the subsequent formation of India and Pakistan, amid a spree of nation-building activities in West Pakistan (present-day Pakistan) and East Pakistan (now Bangladesh), the modern buildings that appeared were single-handedly achieved by Muzharul Islam. He was the senior architect of East Pakistan's government (1958–1964) before opening his own practice Vastukalabid in Dhaka. During his active practice spanning almost four decades (1964–1990s), Islam designed and built universities, public housing, government buildings, institutions, and numerous residences, seeking to derive place-oriented architecture through modern tectonics, environmentally sensitive responses, and the conjunction of cultural typologies with geometric order. His large-scale projects addressed the dichotomy of city and rural realities and suggested alternative ways of urban living. Always in harmony with their natural surroundings, while employing subtle abstraction in the built form and construction details, these works provided functional solutions to social needs. Islam's enduring ideals of Bengali Modernism have served as an ever-present undercurrent, while oscillating between distinct expressions, for inspired architecture in the tropics that transcends local boundaries.

Trained at the University of Oregon (USA), the AA School of Architecture (UK), and Yale University (USA), Muzharul Islam designed buildings that remain iconic to this day. Among many projects, his Institute of Fine Arts at the University of Dhaka, the university's library, and later, the university campuses of Jahangirnagar and Chittagong remain examples of tropical modernism that express time and place. The 1960s also saw the works of a few Western architects and urban planners in this region, such as American Paul Marvin Rudolph (1918–1997), Greek Constantinos A. Doxiadis (1913–1975), and Austrian-American Richard Neutra (1892–1970). Muzharul Islam collaborated with American architect, theorist, and designer Stanley Tigerman (1930–2019) on the design of five polytechnics around the country. Indeed, in the early 1960s, the legendary Louis Kahn (1901–1974) was commissioned to design the parliament complex in Dhaka, which later became one of the most important buildings of the twentieth century and an icon of modern architecture.

The first school of architecture was established in Dhaka in 1962, where American teachers taught in the early years. This first batch of students graduated in 1968, establishing the precedent of locally trained architects in the country. In the early 1970s, there were few practicing architects in Bangladesh and their role in building design was not well understood. A number of early high-rise buildings appeared on the scene in Dhaka, but it was not until the mid-1990s that the practice of architecture was widely understood and gained prominence. By the early 2000s, several local architects were heavily involved in major commissions across Dhaka's cityscape and Rafiq Azam's work began to attract attention.

top
Bangladesh Agriculture University, Mymensingh, 1961
Image courtesy of Paul Marvin Rudolph Archive, Library of Congress

bottom
Bangladesh National Parliament House, Dhaka, 1982
Image courtesy of Flickr Abrinsky

Large shopping centers, office buildings, and housing schemes designed by architects began to appear and were comparable in terms of what was going on elsewhere in the world. For Bangladesh, these developments were "modern" and Dhaka began to look like other cities in South Asia. Tall buildings made of glass, multistory apartment complexes, and retail conglomerates were woven into the visual landscape of the developing city.

At the time, Azam was focused on relatively small-scale projects with a uniquely intimate, curated style that later evolved into his distinctive personal signature, emphasizing the artistic sensibilities and love of land, people, and culture that Muzahrul Islam had so often advocated and demonstrated. Azam's sensitivity to local contexts, sustainable materials, and natural surroundings, in evidence very early on, paved the way for his maturity as an architect who quite literally addresses life on the streets and nurtures Dhaka's spirit and rural origins.

With this city's unbridled spatial growth and its infrastructures in constant flux, the ad hoc skyline is almost unrecognizable with respect to less than a decade ago. Important memories are lost in this rapid rate of change. Community dynamics can transform overnight, along with their social, cultural, and emotional narratives. The conservation of such heritage and knowledge is an important aspect of Rafiq Azam's architectural perspective. His characteristic skyspaces, upper-level "jungles," reminiscent of his childhood garden, and free-flowing spaces, make interaction and seclusion possible at the same time. Indeed, his projects are genuine havens amid the extreme density of the city, allowing neighbors to gather and socialize the way they did in the past. Another vital structural element he has utilized to great effect is the *mer*, a kind of platform found at the front of traditional houses in Old Dhaka, which separates the house from the road but also serves as a place for sitting together with neighbors.

By contrast, houses in new Dhaka have definitive boundary walls demarcating the land. While this is common practice, it does little to establish a link with other residents on the street. In some of his projects in new Dhaka, Azam has actually deconstructed these external walls and replaced them with innovative landscaping elements without solid barriers. This gives welcome relief and creates boundary spaces that facilitate dialogue between passersby and residents in the building. Indeed, Azam has many important buildings to his credit, but his projects in Old Dhaka and his reinterpretations of historic narratives and methods in new Dhaka demonstrate an architectural spirit and prowess that is all his own. Anyone looking at his buildings beyond their functional expressions will recognize the painter in him. His designs reflect the acute sensitivities of an artistic mind: awareness of subtle variations in color, the effects and behavior of light throughout the day, the surface qualities of objects and materials, and the emotional connections to be translated into their work. Azam conceptualizes a building by first doing a watercolor painting in order to define its composition and structure. The sky, water, and indigenous trees that are truly Bangladeshi find abstract expression as each building addresses its surrounding environment. His Mahmoud Residence (1999–2001) and Gulfeshan Apartments (2000–2002) in Dhaka are early examples of his many skillful projects, where greenery and multiple connections

Khazedewan Apartments, Old Dhaka, 2002

to daylight and sky form exterior "social collages" of traditional bricks, handmade ferro-cement tiles, and metal cladding panels that reconnect people with the natural world. Constant traffic, noise, pollution, and a cacophonic existence are evaded by the tranquillity afforded in these homes.

Azam has also designed two Bangladeshi embassies abroad. Representing one's country on such a scale in a foreign land is a huge design challenge. The building has to express important cultural narratives as well as respond to its local environment. For the Bangladesh Chancery Complex in Thimphu (2018–ongoing), Azam is using local materials with strict local building laws to evoke a sense of Bangladesh within its parameters. The prominent use of water to represent his riverine country becomes a compelling visual protagonist against the backdrop of Bhutan's majestic Himalayan landscape. For Pakistan's semi-arid capital of Islamabad, Azam's design of the Bangladesh embassy also features water from which rise slender cylindrical columns. This alludes to the vitality of the countless trees rising above the waterline in the Sundarbans, the world's largest contiguous mangrove forest in Bangladesh, supporting a rich diversity of flora and fauna, including the iconic Bengal tiger.

Mahmood Residence, Uttara, Dhaka, 2001

Brick plinths mark the site's periphery instead of the conventional boundary wall.

As Dhaka grows, its urban areas suffer. Lack of foresight and planning has resulted in environments that are no longer able to meet community needs. Rafiq Azam has turned his attention to such issues, particularly in Old Dhaka, and is literally transforming sites and community lives. For instance, his revitalization of Rasulbagh Shishu Park (children's park), completed in 2021, in Azimpur, Old Dhaka, has become a true beacon of hope in an otherwise underprivileged, high-density neighborhood. Over decades of improper maintenance, persistent flooding, illegal occupation, and antisocial activities, this area covering approximately 2,848 m^2 had not only become a venue for urban mayhem but also a headache and eyesore for its local community. In collaboration with the Dhaka South City Corporation (DSCC), Azam's visionary planning and designs, and sheer persistence, have resulted in a thriving community space that women, children, elders, and neighbors alike can enjoy and belong to. The entire area has come to life, defying the odds.

The Delowar Hossain Area Development (2018–2024) is another example of Azam's team undertaking the redesign and upgrade of a previously derelict area of Old Dhaka. Originally a Hindu-majority area, Muslims began to settle there after the partition of India. The communal harmony that once existed in the area experienced some tension that was relieved by design interventions with local participation. The Hindu crematorium was revitalized with an additional public plaza and prayer spaces for Muslims were also added. Unused buildings were repurposed with community facilities, and the whole area is now an active urban space within a neighborhood that has found new meaning in its social interactions.

Public toilets in Dhaka are inadequate and whatever exists, they are ill-kept and not user-friendly. Azam proposed combining public restroom facilities with other functions such as cafes and eateries or communal facilities. In this way, the premises can be properly maintained and become more accessible. This design solution is simple but well-planned to create a public amenity and restore a sense of shared responsibility.

Alongside his unique practice, Azam has been teaching master classes and leading design workshops in many universities at home and abroad. He has been able to inculcate in students a sense of empathy for the environment. His teaching style is engaging and arouses curiosity about how to design in context. Azam encourages students to learn through his philosophy of respect for the natural world and with a deep understanding of how architectural forms and materials speak for themselves. He believes that learning is enriched not only by observation of local settings but also through travel to other parts of the world. Azam sponsors travel bursaries in a number of universities, where deserving students are offered opportunities to experience other countries and to understand how each society responds to architecture and natural contexts through the observation of history, culture, and, importantly, people. Many students have benefited from his generosity of mind and resources to make them better designers. Rafiq Azam not only designs buildings but also brings back lost memories of urban living in his practice. His projects on regenerating neglected urban areas demonstrate a deep commitment to improving the lives of the people. He devotes his time and resources to nurturing young minds, so that they, like him, can help build better living environments.

water as land

CONVERSATION
ROSA MARIA FALVO & RAFIQ AZAM

part one

RMF

Bangladesh has undergone huge changes since you were a child on the streets of Old Dhaka. We have worked together for almost fifteen years now and I know that your life as an architect is a very personal odyssey, involving countless obstacles and requiring tremendous flexibility, resilience, and a deep sense of purpose on your part. What keeps you going?

RA

The metaphor of an odyssey is a good one. There have been many challenges and also triumphs. But I feel that I am always gaining momentum in my original mission to provide architecture for "green living." It keeps me committed to this profession. Even though we are in a very chaotic city, I want to restore our friendship with the natural world. Designing is a journey, allowing me to creatively materialize dreams, like being an artist, which is the difficult part. I'm really focused on bringing natural processes and elements into nature-starved urban areas and developing positive solutions for people. It's always a search for balance.

RMF

This new book is unique in many ways, but for me, the most exciting part is that it affords international audiences the chance to appreciate your insider perspectives in the public sector. Your approach is representative of your cultural context, but it also specifically responds to some of the extreme problems you face, even daily. You're working on a true legacy and I'm very happy to be involved, especially at this transitional time in world history. The Subcontinent is literally metamorphizing in front of our very eyes, and you have to communicate, educate, and collaborate all at the same time on so many levels within Bangladeshi society. Looking over your career so far, what would you say has inspired you?

RA

It took a lot of time for me to really understand my role and what architecture can be. Since I had never actually resolved to become an architect from the start—I wanted to be an artist—my ambiguity led me to want both. I feel that they're actually siblings, always intertwining with each other, and I realized that architecture is like a courtyard—an empty space—and you need to fill it with life. Everything, even a tree, encloses this empty space, collecting stories, events, the downpours, the winds, and the mutable skies. I also realized it's like three-dimensional poetry. Since this profession is about humanity and human-centric activities and feelings, I believe you have to educate yourself across the arts: literature, painting, cinema, and so forth, alongside the sciences and the technologies, to have a chance at understanding something about our complex relationships with our environments, other people, and what actually nurtures kinship.

Early on, I attended workshops on Rabindranath Tagore's magnificent verses, novels, short stories, and dramas, studying his reflections on society, humanity, love, respect, and conflict. Similarly, I also pondered the life of Rama in the *Ramayana*, India's great Sanskrit epic by the sage Valmiki. I was attracted to the post–World War II Theatre of the Absurd, especially

Rabindranath Tagore by Georges Chevalier, 1926
Courtesy of Musée Départemental Albert-Kahn, Boulogne-Billancourt, France

Rabindranath Tagore (1861–1941) was a Bengali polymath who worked as a poet, writer, playwright, composer, philosopher, social reformer, and painter of the Bengal Renaissance. In 1913, he became the first non-European to win a Nobel Prize in any category, and also the first lyricist to win the Nobel Prize in Literature.

Samuel Beckett's *Waiting for Godot*, as well as Franz Kafka's timeless protagonists, facing such bizzare predicaments and absurdly bureaucratic powers. And I have always been fascinated with how you can change the human environment and transform almost everything, even dramatically; how things connect and disconnect; how the sun moves, with the incline of its winter light in the northern hemisphere, and how it's just diametrically opposite in the southern hemisphere. I'm constantly looking out for the wind, where it's coming from and where it's going, and how much water we receive each year. In Bangladesh, the water spans an area of more than two million square kilometers, just above the Himalayas, and flows down to meet us through the Ganges and the Brahmaputra basins.

top
Rice cultivation on the salt flats of southern Bangladesh, 2007

bottom
Sadarghat Port, Dhaka, 2009

Imagery on pp. 72–73, courtesy of Rosa Maria Falvo

RMF

This is certainly a uniquely deltic land. It's literally configured by these massive water bodies. It has land borders with India to the north, west, and east, and with Myanmar to the southeast. There's the coastline along the Bay of Bengal to the south, it's separated from Bhutan and Nepal in the north by the Siliguri Corridor, and also from China by the Indian state of Sikkim. I jokingly call it the showerhead of the world!

RA

Well, geographically, all this water is our "land," and we're acutely aware of its power and influence, even within these city walls.In fact, the area around Dhaka consists of a flat plain bound by the Dhaleswari, Buriganga, and Sitalakhya rivers. This in turn creates a network that streams into the mighty Meghna, Padma (Ganges), and Jamuna (Brahmaputra) rivers. Bangladesh is actually bisected by the Tropic of Cancer, so it's defined by its monsoon climate, with distinctly dry and wet seasons. Our coastal areas are influenced by the Bay of Bengal, which means high humidity and cyclones, but the temperate north is under the realm of the great Himalayan Mountains, which provide cooler temperatures. So I incorporate green infrastructure, like vegetated rooftops, roadside and courtyard plantings, absorbent gardens, and other measures to capture, filter, and somehow harvest or manage these rains.

Tremendous rivers mold every aspect of this richly fertile land, not only its physiography but also our way of life. We're always dealing with constant and often rapid changes, even spectacular extremes. If we could only imagine ourselves as fish living here, it might change our whole approach to our country—our urban planning, our economy, and our technology. It should all be connected and working with the water. Instead, we started building roads and elevated expressways, and we continue to build anything we want on and above the ground, thinking the water is our enemy, pushing it away, which is, ultimately, impossible. Basically, we have declared war on the very waters that feed us, and that inevitably leads to suffering, which will continue unless we change our attitudes. So this is all about understanding what best-practice architecture and planning can actually achieve for us and our long-term potential.

RMF
Your work is deeply rooted in Bengali heritage, but you're also profoundly influenced by your travels throughout Asia and the rest of the world.

RA
Yes, and one important early influence was a master class I did in Australia with renowned Australian architect Glenn Murcutt, back in 2004. His climate-sensitive designs really resonate with my own desire to establish "green living." His wonderful ethos of "touching the Earth lightly" might be materialized in Australia's fantastic landscapes—vast, undulating flat plains and slopes—but most of Bangladesh hovers less than 12 meters above sea level, while the next big storm hangs on the horizon. This land can even disappear if the climate changes more dramatically. So there's some logic to building high-rises here, especially with our dense population, but using a light touch is very challenging! I still believe we should be looking at strategies like floating houses and things like that, allowing the water and the winds to pass through. But even so, there are instances where we simply need tall buildings, so we must work hard to recover lost vegetation. For instance, in my design for the Dipu Sharmin Residence in Nikunja, one of the most coveted areas of Dhaka, we had to deal with a relatively small plot and strict height restrictions. So we decided to build below ground, on the principle that "every floor can be the ground floor" while ensuring that natural light could enter as much as possible. As the house rises up, it reveals more and more untamed, tropical greenery on each level, as well as artistic references in the decor, to make each living space a tropical sanctuary in the middle of the city.

RMF
So you effectively redistributed the vegetation.

RA
Yes, exactly, and achieved much more than the usual total greenery that could be expected—perhaps even double. This gave us the satisfaction of not just saving the green or acting responsibly, but rather creating something new to re-establish its vital functions and our innate psychological connection to it. Of course, orientation is very important, and there are thousands of years' worth of typological maxims in our country instructing us to have the house facing south; that north is very unhealthy; that water bodies should be in the east and bamboo bushes in the west, screening the hot sun. If we consider this kind of ancient knowledge on the "science of living," we can find our winter sun, shun its intensity during the summer, and still benefit from the winds arriving from the south, southeast, and southwest. All these ideas are very important to us.

top
Transporting logs, Chittagong, 2008

bottom
Buriganga River ("Old Ganges") in Dhaka, 2009

Lalon Shah (c.1772–1890) was a renowned Bengali spiritual leader, philosopher, mystic poet, and social reformer. An icon of Bengali culture, he inspired many philosophers, poets, and social thinkers, including Rabindranath Tagore and Kazi Nazrul Islam.

It is said that Jyotirindranath Tagore (1849–1925), a Bengali playwright, musician, editor, painter, and the younger brother of Rabindranath Tagore, sketched this only portrait of Lalon in 1889 in his houseboat on the Padma River.
Image courtesy of Indian National Museum

RMF
Using Laugier's "primitive hut" principles and the latest technology at the same time.

RA
Of course, we have to test and re-test the efficacy of ancient practices and ideas within our current technological and climatic realities, but I think all these considerations define good architecture. To address some of our challenges, this country has taken the lead in climate adaptative efforts, investing in flood-resistant infrastructure, early warning systems, mangrove restoration, and floating farms to help communities cope with extreme weather. There are attempts to implement large-scale embankment projects and even climate migration strategies to protect the most vulnerable. But we are still one of the most "at-risk" nations in the world when sea levels rise.

So, we should be at the cutting edge of critical thinking about how much we're taking from the water, our land, and the space we have left, and how much we're restoring all of them; what can be reused and remodeled, and what needs to be reorganized and regained. Basically, it's about creating empty spaces for nature, for people, for birds, and for butterflies. The much-debated Anthropocene and our current "Great Acceleration" mark our egoistic drive to dominate each other and the planet. Architecture is central to that, in the name of civilization. We can now finally admit that we are just part of the infinitely larger cycles.

RMF
Your mastery of light, water, and air has been compared to poetic expressions. So it appears that at heart you're still a painter who uses architecture as his medium, fusing tradition, landscape, and mysticism.

RA
You could say that. I always say I'm a painter by conviction and an architect by destiny. My journey began with a compromise between my love for drawing and my father's aspirations for me to pursue a more traditional career. Over time, I realized that architecture is far more than producing functional structures—it's essentially storytelling, navigating people's emotions, and weaving together the light and space.

Bangladesh's natural beauty and its resilient people have always influenced my paintings. Immediately after the Liberation War, when I was still in primary school, my elder brother found a box of Winsor & Newton watercolors in a neighboring house that had been abandoned by a Pakistani family who once lived there. The house had already been looted but this magical box remained, so I took it home, despite our father's strict instructions to stay away from such loot. Since I was born and raised in the historic center of Dhaka, my subjects were clearly urban, focusing on streets, alleyways, and buildings. It wasn't until I started traveling to the villages on the outskirts of Dhaka that I began expanding my purview and love for the beauty of my homeland. This created in me a sort of urban-rural juxtaposition that gradually appeared in my artwork.

RMF
I know from experience that many of the spaces you have designed exude a meditative quality. How do you achieve this effect?

RA
I believe architecture should nurture the soul. One of my most cherished childhood memories is sitting in our courtyard, watching the shadows dance on moonlit nights. That experience, like a kind of make-believe theater, has shaped my whole approach to design that aims to evoke tranquility. My passion for architecture was very much fed by the great teachers Muzharul Islam, Basirul Haque, Shamsul Wares and Uttam Kumar Saha, for instance, but my heart and mind have always sought the language of "nowness"—that representation of the contemporary, what it means to exist in our time, and how we can express ourselves uniquely within it. Through my earlier projects like the Meghna Residence (2003–2005) in Dhanmondi, I explored the threshold between my learning and unlearning. So my formal academic training was subdued by my emotional responses to Bengali Romanticism, with water bodies, untamed greenery, summer breezes, and so forth.

For the SA Residence (2005–2011) in Gulshan, I delved more deeply into the songs of our great Baul Lalon Shah. His verses strongly advocate for humanism over any religious or societal divisions—emphasizing unity, equality, and peace. I find his philosophy very enriching, the way he effortlessly integrated everything, including Hinduism, Tantric Buddhism, and Sufi Islam, into one unique spiritual discourse. Lalon described the constant, interdependent dialogue between body and mind. So I see architecture as a physical body—a shell—and nature as its mind and its soul.

RMF
What challenges do Bangladeshi architects face in highly urbanized Dhaka?

RA
This unbridled pace needs to bring wisdom and historical experience back into the picture to restore some balance between density and livability. My pivot toward "green architecture" in 1995 predated this movement's rise and intuitively stemmed from my artistic sensibilities. I realized that thinking with nature in my designs and buildings was not just a preference or about decoration, but rather an intense calling.

RMF
If you had to describe good architecture in just one word, what would it be?

RA
Harmony.

homeostasis

DIPU SHARMIN RESIDENCE

Nikunja, Dhaka

2013–2016

This single-family residential building consists of four stories above ground and one below, oriented southward along a "T" junction road. Its design effectively harnesses consistent summer breezes predominantly from the southeast while allowing ample winter light from the low angle of the sun. This southward orientation also provides enhanced views of distant trees. The vertical design plays a crucial and strategic role, connecting the basement and ground floor into a unified guest area through a double-height space that invites sunlight deep into the basement.

The objective here was to establish both horizontal and vertical connections within the entire home, emphasizing the integration of greenery on various levels. Trees from the neighboring northern bus depot also create a visual link, intertwining with the living spaces, functional areas, and other natural elements, ultimately transforming the architecture into a verdant oasis. Due to its proximity to Dhaka International Airport, height restrictions cap the building at 13 meters. This limitation inspired an innovative subterranean design that accommodates living areas, entertainment zones, and recreational facilities while still maximizing all the natural light.

The incorporation of vegetation on every floor fosters a deeper connection with nature, creating a homeostatic ambiance. The ground floor features a blend of cultivated and wild greenery, with layered and established vertical gardens that ensure each level feels like an extension of the ground floor. Primarily constructed with shear concrete walls, this design addresses the seismic conditions of Dhaka while making a strong architectural statement that is rooted in concrete.

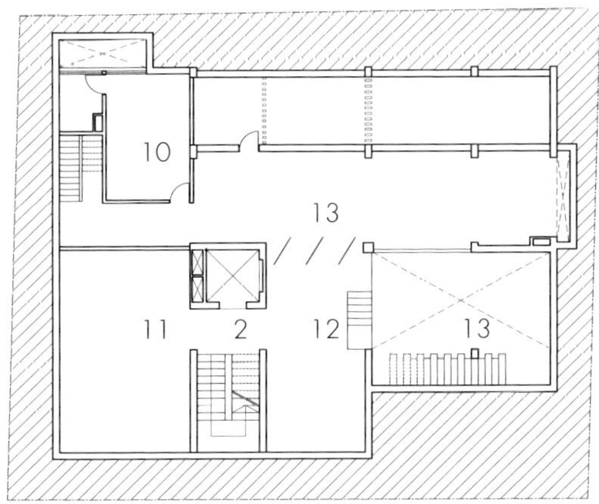

Basement Plan

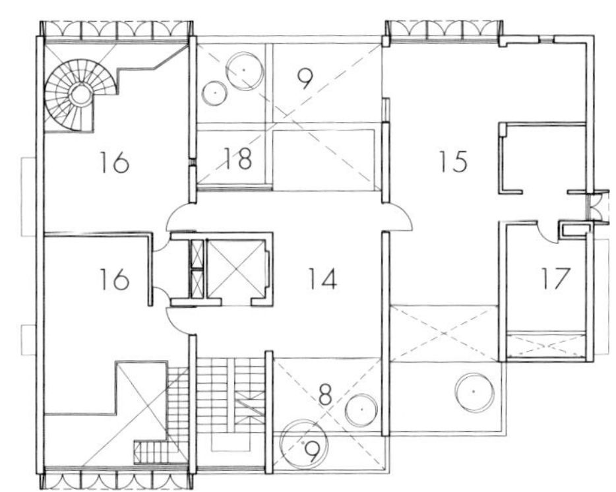

2nd-Floor Plan

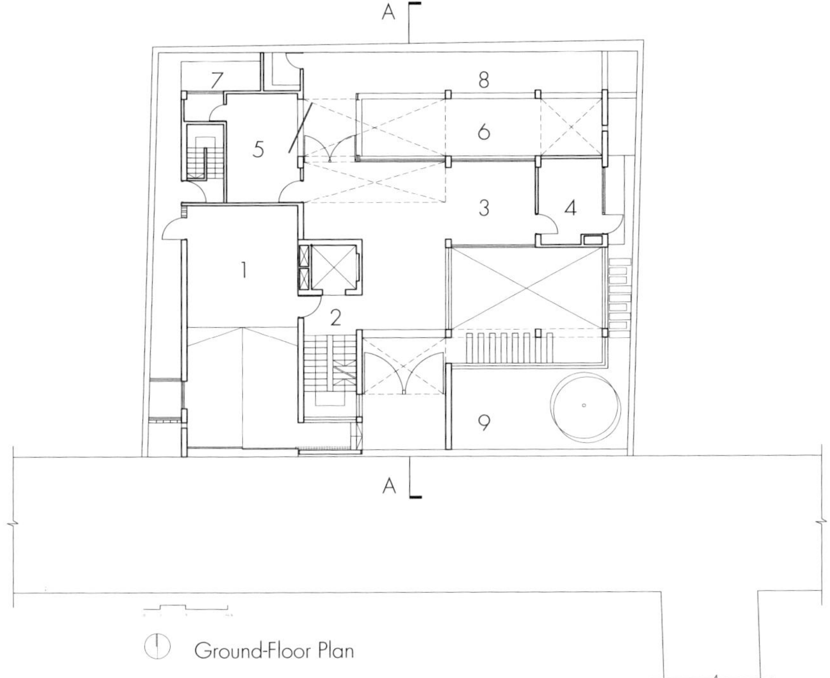

Ground-Floor Plan

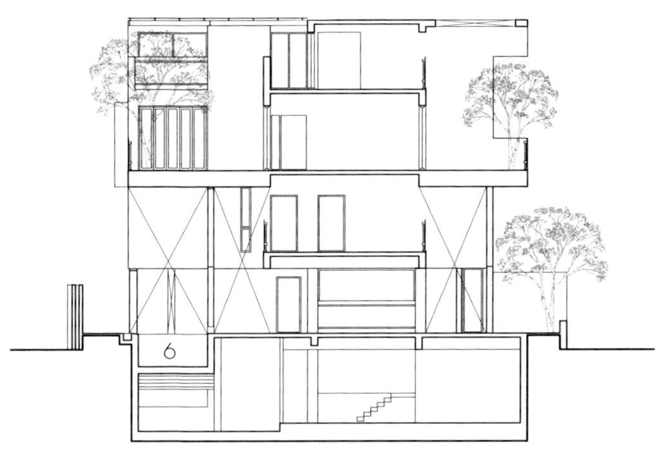

Section AA

1. parking
2. lobby
3. dining room
4. kitchen
5. study
6. pool
7. shower
8. deck
9. garden
10. staff room
11. movie theater
12. sitting room
13. formal living room
14. family living room
15. master bedroom
16. bedroom
17. bathroom
18. water body

previous page
View from the road on the south.

following pages
North courtyard on the third level.

Light entering the basement living space.

following pages
Rooftop garden

permeability

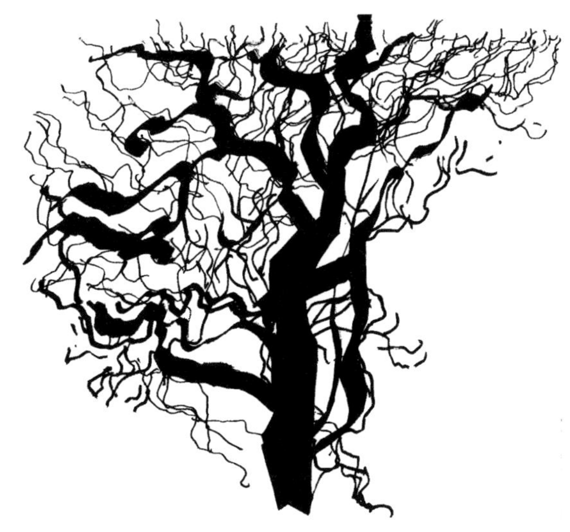

ASIF ZAHIR RESIDENCE

Gulshan, Dhaka

2017–2020

Nestled in the vibrant heart of Gulshan, this residence is a five-story single-family home, with each floor designed for a distinct function. The first two levels of the space are characterized by thoughtfully designed entertainment areas that exude warmth and sophistication, effectively inviting guests to engage in a refined social experience. The third level serves as a cozy retreat for the young couple, combining modern aesthetics with comfort, while the fourth level is a tranquil sanctuary for their mother, designed to promote relaxation and well-being.

At the top, the fifth level boasts a bright gymnasium and a versatile multipurpose hall, leading to an open-air landscaped area with a shallow water feature that reflects the sky's changing hues. A west-facing oculus captures stunning sunsets and adds to the ambiance.

Mature trees enhance the views in the eastern and southeastern areas, while a beautifully landscaped lawn in the southeast corner emphasizes the home's unique "L" shape. This design promotes a seamless connection to nature, giving the impression of a structure that is gracefully floating against the expansive monsoon sky.

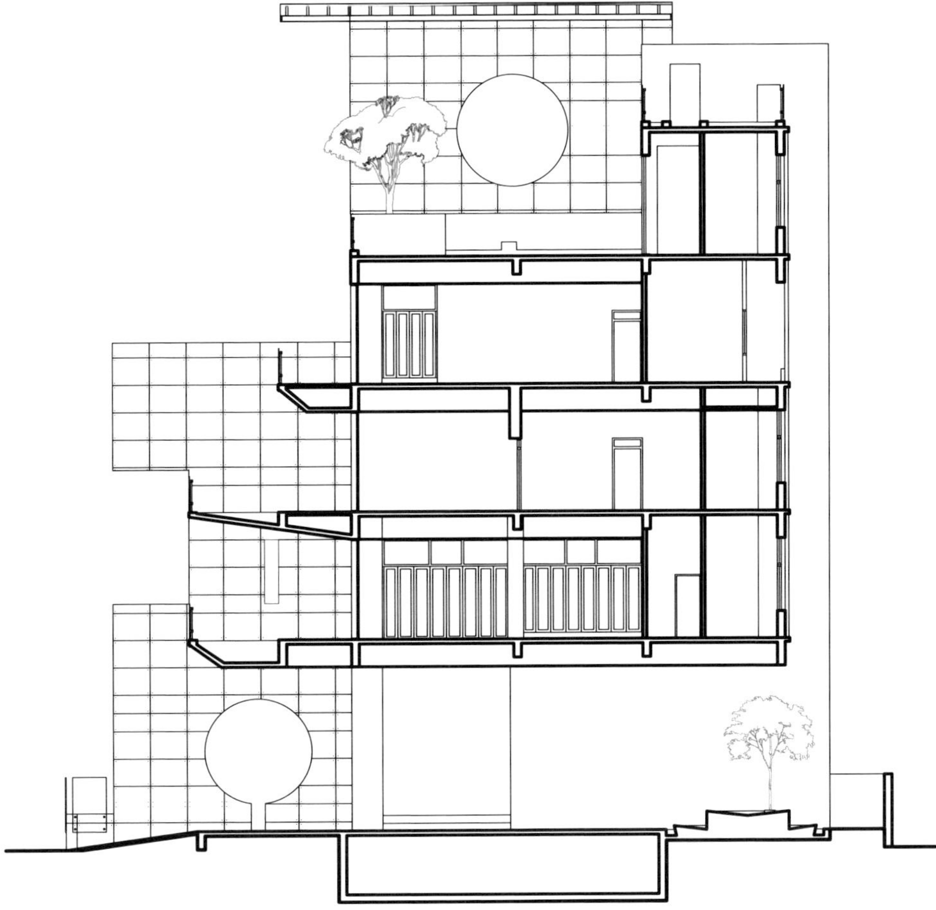

Section AA

previous page
Eastern lawn on the ground level.

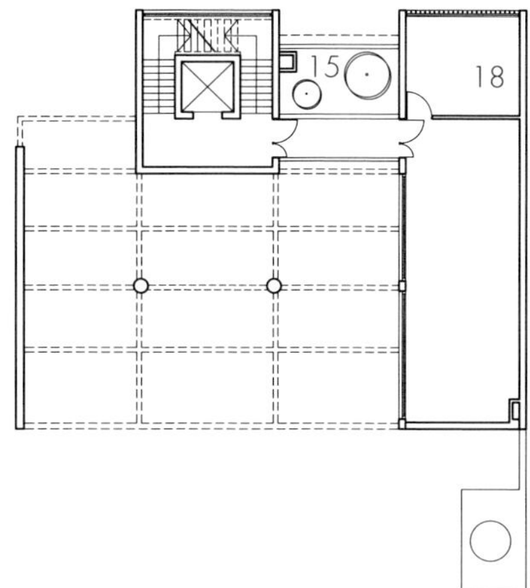

5th-Floor Plan

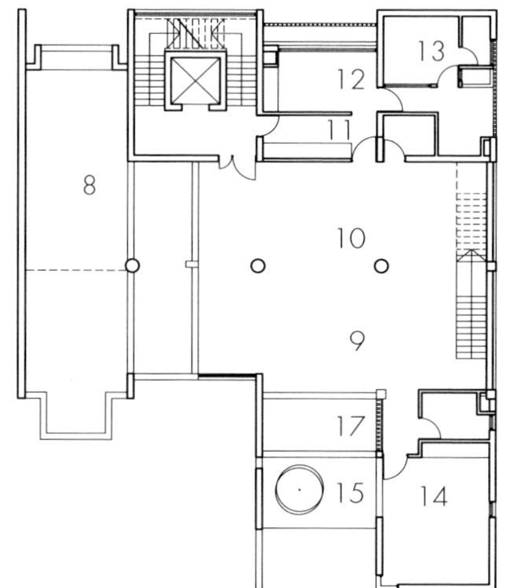

1st-Floor Plan

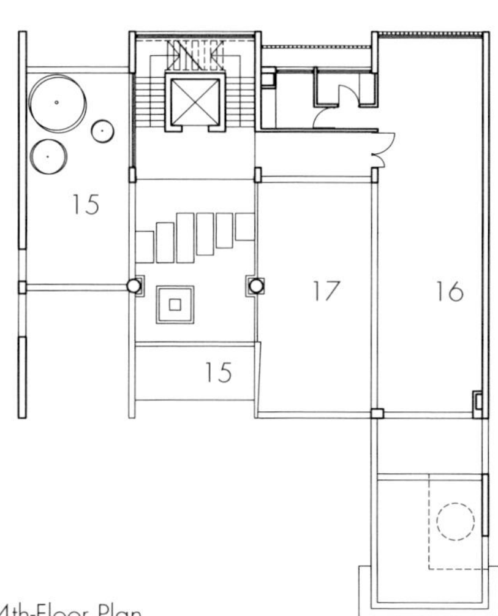

4th-Floor Plan

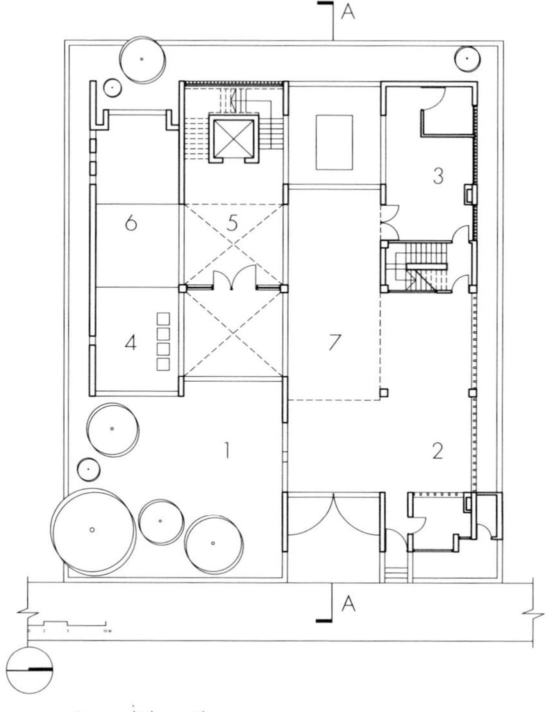

Ground-Floor Plan

1. east lawn
2. parking
3. substation
4. water body
5. foyer
6. sitting room
7. car drop area
8. pool
9. dining room
10. formal living room
11. dry kitchen
12. wet kitchen
13. staff room
14. guest bedroom
15. garden
16. hall and gym
17. terrace
18. mechanical room

next page
Sky through the rooftop oculus.

Asif Zahir Residence in context.

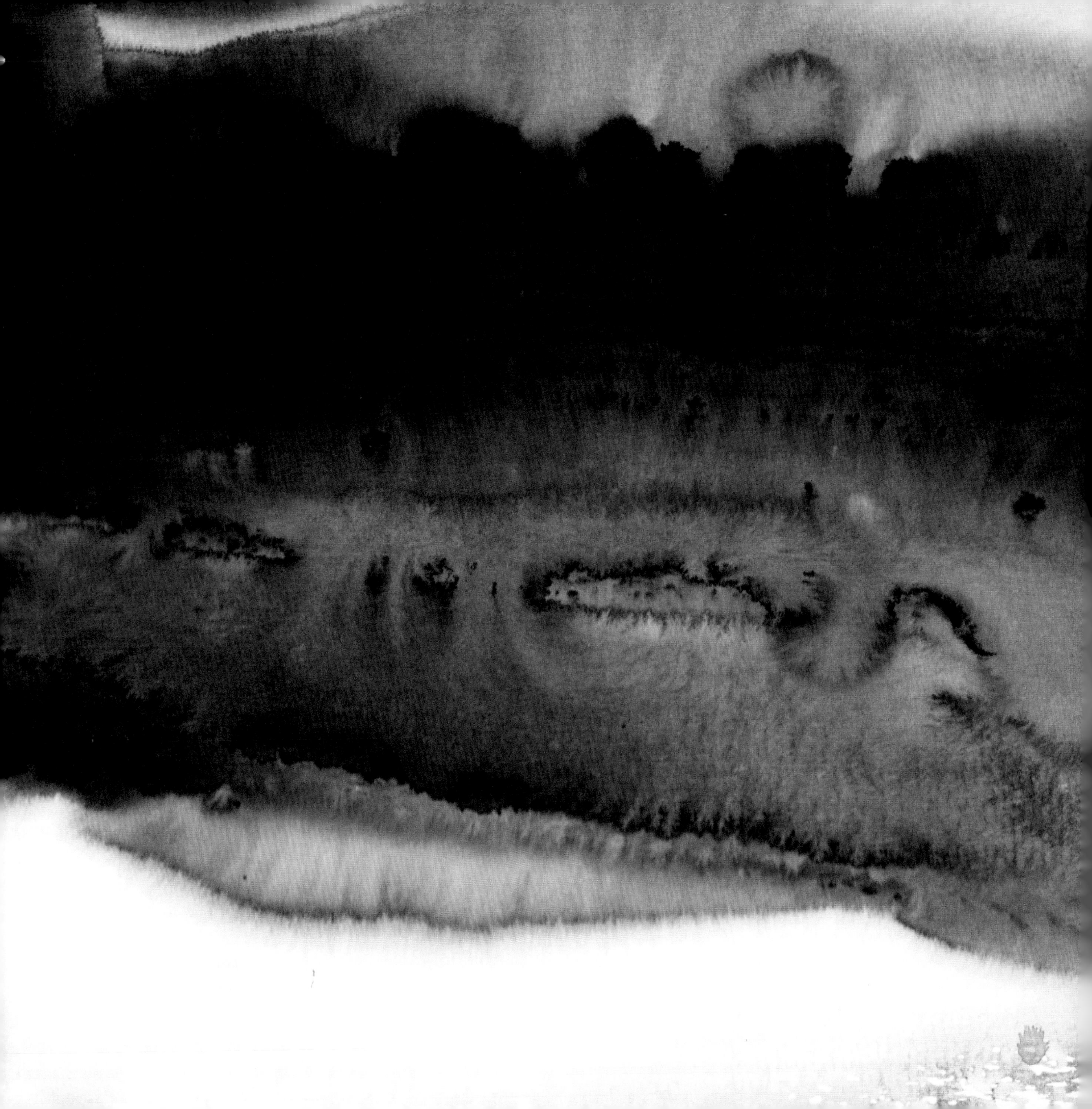

social sculpture

HAQUE'S SOUTH LEAF

Gulshan, Dhaka

2017–2021

For this ambitious residential project built on the owner's land and previous family home, the artistic intention was to design something unconventional, giving a sculptural quality to the built form and not merely its functionality and comforts. The owner's memories provided a rich source of inspiration and the plastic capabilities of the concrete were exploited for creative purpose and structural necessity in this fourteen-story building. The orthogonal geometry was injected with acute angles to achieve a sense of curvature as is reflected in the subtle notations of Eastern music.

With a community hall and pool, spa facilities, twenty-four apartments, two basements, and thirty-six parking spaces, this building is nestled in a quiet area of Gulshan. With prominent column structures, terracotta brick infill, and numerous green balconies, its design draws full benefit from its southeast corner, allowing for ample wind during the summer and winter sunlight. Each level has two four-bedroom simplexes fitted with verandas and gardens along the southeast side that safeguard their glass windows and are positioned to screen afternoon heat. Mr. Haque's home on the twelfth-floor is fitted with a balcony and extended green terrace. This generous duplex retains a connection between the land and the sky with panoramic views of the cityscape. The ground floor is enclosed by a horizontal grille and vegetation wall to seamlessly connect the space to the rest of the city. This medley of wind and light, and the rippling silence of water, echoes the final peace achieved after the country's victory during the 1971 Liberation War. The transformation of chaos and pain affords a uniquely poetic expression to this contemporary urban sculpture.

Eliptical void at the entrance.

HAQUE'S SOUTH LEAF

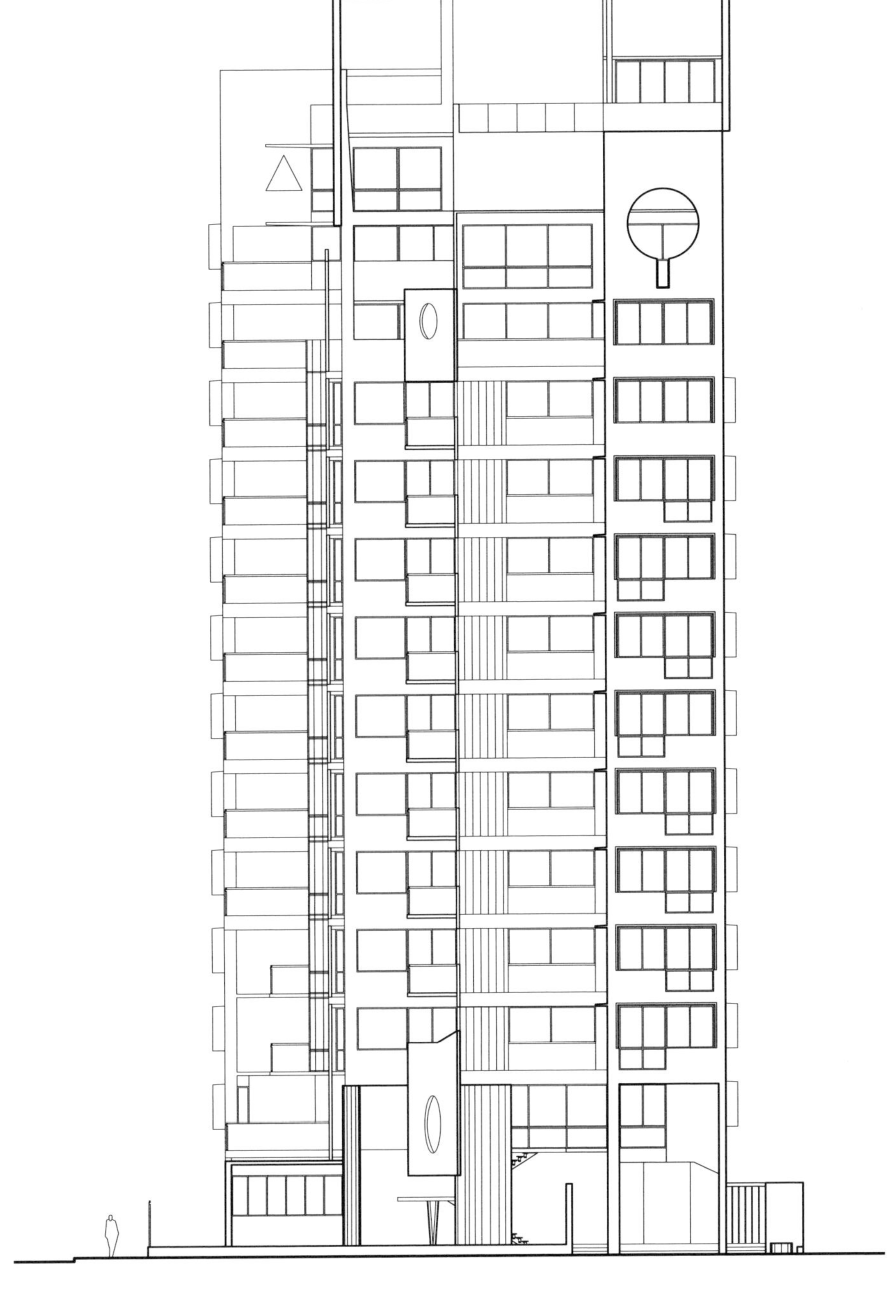

East Elevation

metallic prose

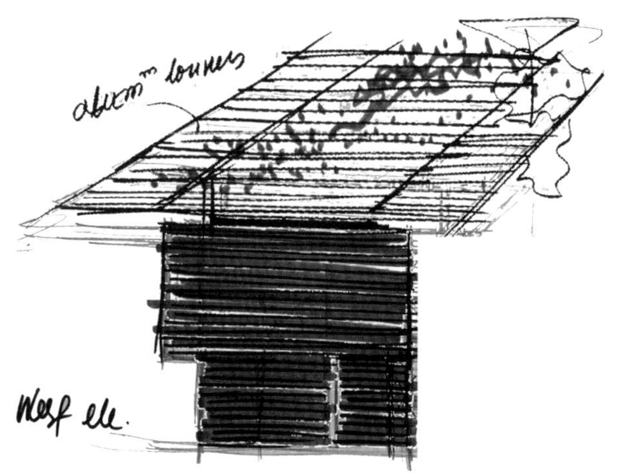

SHADHIN RESIDENCE

Bashundhara Residential Area, Dhaka

2019–2024

In the heart of the nineteenth century, the Industrial Revolution sparked a remarkable transformation across the globe, reshaping societies and economies in ways that would forever alter the course of history. It was intended to create more freedom and encourage people to ask questions and solve more problems. This set off a chain of events that compelled communities, on the one hand, to focus on acquiring essential resources needed to navigate a new era, and on the other, to fall victim to diminishing social coherence.

The concept for this residence was to blend Bengali cultural elements with industrial materials like metal, to create an ambiance of tropical postindustrial romanticism. The design drew inspiration from its 608.51 m^2 corner plot, which features a small urban jungle at the junction of two roads, serving as a starting point for engaging with the land.

This seven-story residential building accommodates an extended family, with the ground and second floors dedicated to guest accommodations, while the upper levels house the owner and his parents. The top floor also includes a compact home office, a garden, and an area for drying clothes. To achieve this, cascading gardens were layered in to elevate the whole structure. A large metal frame with louvers was introduced to soften the verticality of this house, while also screening the morning sunlight and preventing a greenhouse effect inside. This metal trellis promotes interaction between light and greenery, enhancing the overall spatial quality of the environment. As a result, the residence has become a sanctuary for birds and humans alike.

Metalic trellis with louvers.

previous page
Morning light on the northern elevation.

Twilight on the eastern elevation.

following page
Terrace and garden intertwine on the third level.

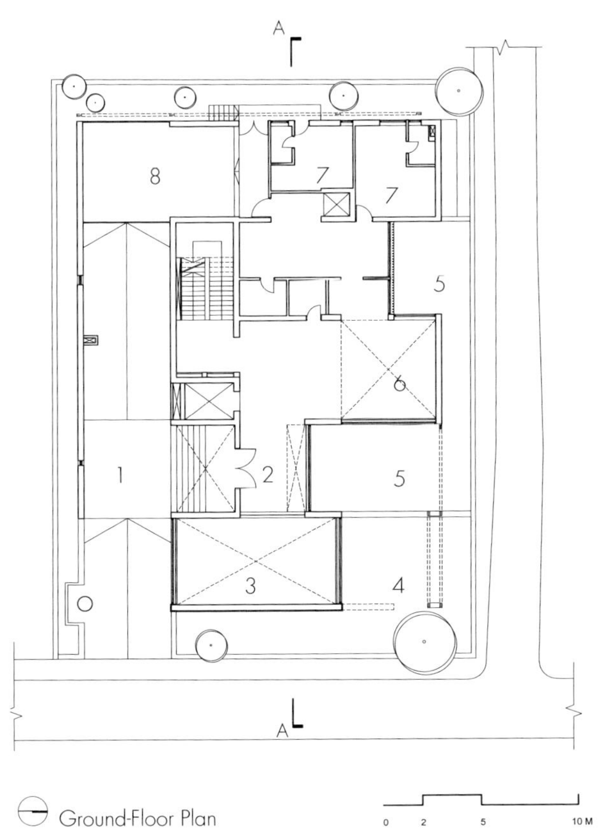

Ground-Floor Plan

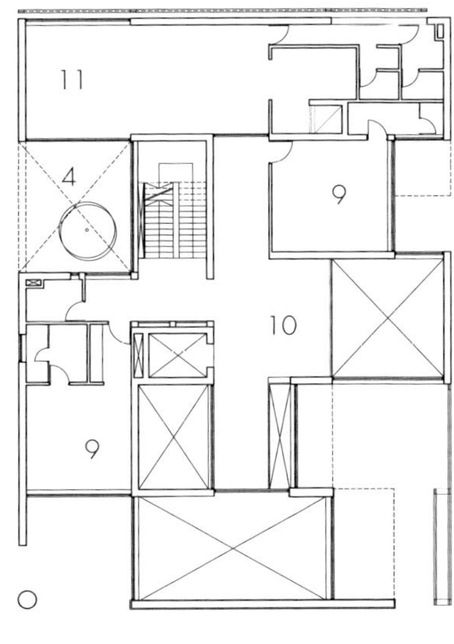

1st-Floor Plan

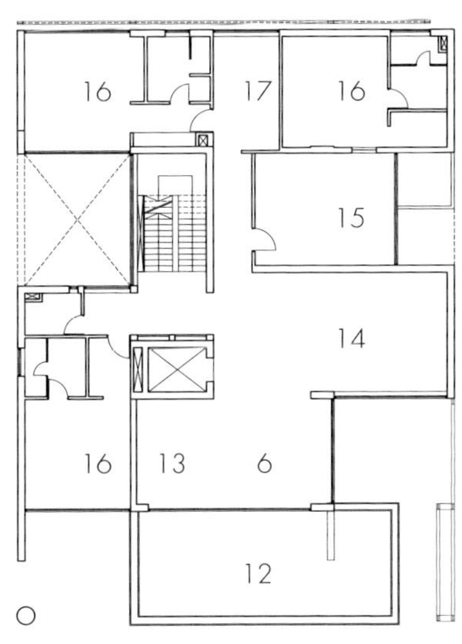

2nd-Floor Plan

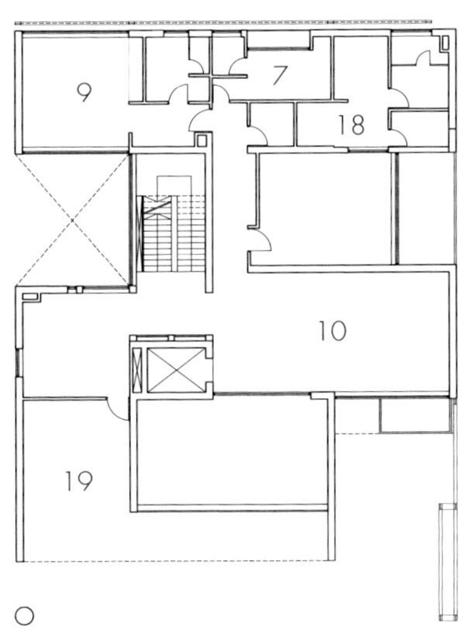

3rd-Floor Plan

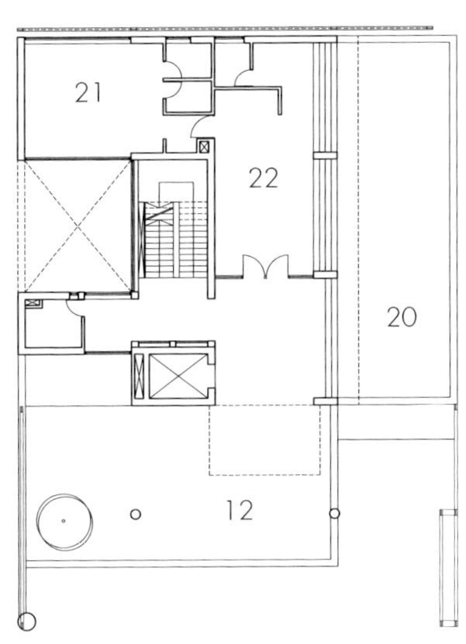

4th-Floor Plan

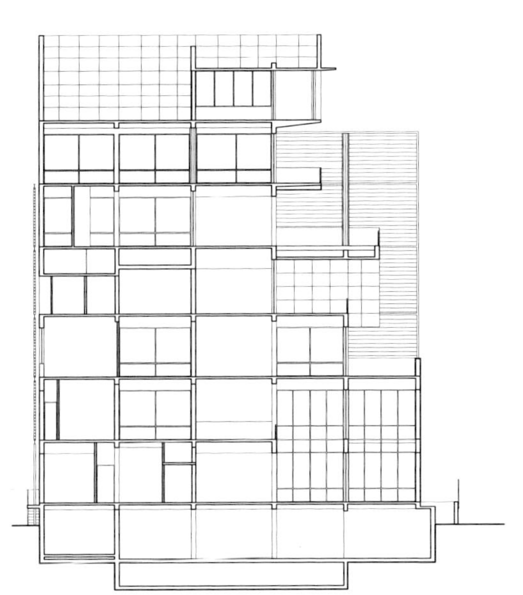

Section AA

1. car drop area
2. foyer
3. living room
4. garden
5. water body
6. dining room
7. staff room
8. mechanical room
9. guest bedroom
10. lounge room
11. entertainment area
12. terrace and garden
13. open kitchen
14. family living room
15. master bedroom
16. children's bedroom
17. play area
18. prayer room
19. library
20. pool
21. gym
22. bar

previous page
Formal living room on the ground level.

Penumbra on the fifth level.

next page
Layered greenery on each level.

Northeastern view from the road.

previous page
Swimming pool on the rooftop.

BEYOND BORDERS
PHILIP GOAD

local and international

The strength and vibrancy of architecture cultures across the globe wax and wane. They have done so for centuries. Internal circumstances of politics, civil conflict, economic growth, social upheaval, colonization and decolonization, and networks of patronage among a host of other factors all contribute. There are also often moments when the emergence of a new generation of young architects coincides with a particular moment in a nation's history, a productive cultural spur to action. Such is the case in Bangladesh over the past twenty years. A group of extremely talented architects, most graduating between 1980 and 1995, and, significantly, most educated within architecture schools located in Bangladesh, has emerged. They are confident, worldly, mobile, and articulate. Many, individually or as a group, have been published internationally, been the subject of and participants in exhibitions, and invited to speak across the globe. But they are also critical, ethically committed, and acutely self-aware of the place in which they work and live, and how their work is perceived.

Rafiq Azam and his practice Shatotto sit within this group, which includes practitioners like Marina Tabassum, Kashef Chowdhury, and the academic Kazi Khaleed Ashraf among others. But Azam is different. He is neither the oldest of the group nor the youngest, but he is of that group, arguably, the most prolific and hence by extension, the most successful and, I would argue, the one treading the hardest and finest of lines. This is because of his willingness to participate in the difficult challenges of what it means to practice in Bangladesh today and by extension in South and Southeast Asia in the first half of the twenty-first century. It is also because his work does not automatically fit within conventional, arguably Eurocentric, understandings of the "artist-architect," the savvy commercial practitioner, the not-for-profit sector, or the anonymous institutional public servant working on behalf of the government. Nor does Azam position his work so exclusively according to any one "type" of practitioner or practice. Yet it is precisely this capacity to work across different scales of commission, budget, and conceptual aesthetics that has allowed his practice to cross multiple borders—socially, geographically, and internationally. This makes Azam therefore unusual and distinctive within the South Asian region—as a Bangladeshi architect with projects not just across Bangladesh but also in Pakistan, Bhutan, and Malaysia. One of the few architects to have achieved a similar regional message of exceptional quality and explored across national borders in this region was the late Australian expatriate architect Kerry Hill (1943–2018). Based in Singapore, his practice gained that distinction largely through the international networks of hotels and resorts, especially through the Aman chain.[1] And it was and remains a sensibility drawn from his early experiences in Bali rather than—as with Azam—the product of a deeply personal design growth with its basis in his home city. For Azam, Dhaka is central to his personal psyche and his approach to architecture.[2]

Part of the contemporary relevance of Azam's work is that its references and inspirations are intrinsically of its region and place—not Europe and not the United States. While at a personal level, Azam acknowledges a respectful debt to the legacy of Le Corbusier and Louis Kahn's magisterial works in the Indian sub-continent, for him this is never genuflection nor elemental emulation. Nor is this debt overplayed or overstated. In short, he has moved on—while others

have not. Instead, Azam's critical intellectual context is found within contemporary practice in his own region. For example, Azam knows and admires the concrete work of Japanese architect Tadao Ando and the landscape directives of Australian architect Glenn Murcutt.[3] But again, for Azam, these are lessons of approach rather than tactics of quotation. What is important here in terms of materiality, for example, is that Azam is acutely aware of the possibilities and limits of concrete construction in the region and the intrinsic part it plays in the local construction industry, "Third World" labor practices, its weathering properties, and its seismic benefits—Dhaka ranks, for example, as one of the twenty cities most vulnerable to earthquakes. That concrete now is under scrutiny for its challenge to sustainability is a question for the greater construction industry globally, especially given its widespread, some might say unwavering, application across the developing world.[4]

Over the last ten years, Azam's design palette has consolidated to become truly his own, with an increased range of expertise in different building typologies and different urban scales. This expanded repertoire is what today further separates Azam and his firm from his contemporaries. Within Dhaka alone, recent projects like the urban ensembles of parks, playing fields, and community buildings like Rasulbagh Shishu Park (2018–2021) and the Shahid Haji Abdul Alim Playground (2017–2019) stitch together and reinvigorate communities at the local level and across multiple generations. These are places not just where children claim, in David Harvey's words, "the right to the city" but also places claimed by women and the elderly.[5] These projects are defined by their shared urban spaces, open to everyone. The inclusion of plants, trees, and hard landscaping, and the correcting of water management systems, means that these projects also become permanent "green lungs," key moments of urban regeneration. If the street stalls that were once there have been displaced—informal places of exchange that often gave a serendipitous and messy vitality to the existing urban setting—the question has to be asked. What is the balance between loss and gain? Informality will make its way back but now, what Azam, his collaborators, and the community have done is ensure the urban balance is in favor of greater amenity for a greater number, and for the greater good. Like the hundreds of pocket-size playgrounds that Dutch architect Aldo van Eyck designed for postwar Amsterdam between 1947 and 1978 as an act of urban remediation, almost like a form of urban weaving where each project merges with the city, Azam's ambition with these community projects is to restore a form of human dignity to the urban chaos that is modern Dhaka.[6] These projects in Bangladesh are much larger and more complex than Van Eyck's in Amsterdam. They take more time, and, as an architect, Azam must move beyond conventional professional borders and work with many players, within demanding bureaucratic settings, and with different ethnic and religious communities. Not easy. The Delowar Hossain Area Development and Crematorium (2018–2024), located in one of the city's most depressed and polluted areas right next to the Buriganga River, involved careful negotiation with both Muslim and Hindu communities, the restoration of the Hindu crematorium pond, the creation of a public plaza, shaded steps and seating areas, and open play spaces for children of all ages, as well as a new, pyramid-roofed brick crematorium structure. The transformation has been remarkable: another of Dhaka's urban "villages" now has a new and harmonious heart.

top
Aman Kyoto, Kyoto, Japan, 2019
Kerry Hill Architects.
Image courtesy of Nacása & Partners Inc.

bottom
Playground, Buskenblaserstraat,
Amsterdam, Netherlands, circa 1947
Architect Aldo Van Eyck.
Image courtesy of Amsterdam City Archive

The expansion of Azam's architectural remit has also seen Shatotto complete institutional buildings of distinction. These are not just mature architectural statements but also significant contributions to the development and increasing sophistication of contemporary Islamic architecture culture across the Levant, the Middle East, the Indian subcontinent, and Southeast Asia. What Azam brings to these buildings is not only the typological constants inherent to Islamic ritual but also a very particular Bengali preoccupation with materiality and, especially in Dhaka, architectural questions of water, light, and shade. The Aga Khan Academy Phase 1, with Feilden Clegg Bradley Studios (2022) and the Mayor Mohammad Hanif Jame Mosque (2016–2018) extend earlier contributions of architects like Hassan Fathy in Egypt, Rasem Badran in Jordan and Saudi Arabia, and Yuswadi Saliya in Indonesia that champion vernacular Islamic architectural traditions as living and relevant languages—not just symbolically but also climatically—for the making of buildings. The use, for example, of bricks, a venerable and sustainable building tradition in Bengal for thousands of years, sacred geometries in plan and detail, and allusions that meld the similar spatial concepts of open courtyarded Buddhist Mahaviharas (centers of learning) with the *madrasa* (Islamic school), inform the Aga Khan Academy's formal organization.

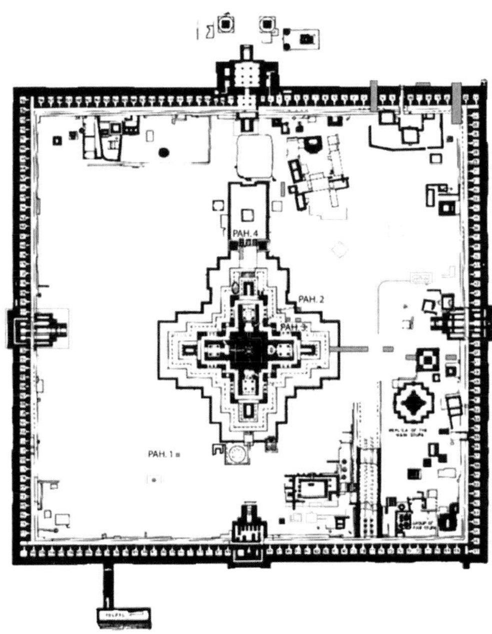

Master plan of Somapura Mahavihara, Naogaon District, Bangladesh, constructed in the late eighth century CE under the patronage of the Pala King Dharmapala. Image courtesy of Indian Culture Portal, Government of India

Similarly, Azam's Hanif Jame Mosque next to the Azimpur graveyard in Lalbagh, is a convincing reimagining of the canons of Islamic religious architecture. Each critical component of the traditional mosque—minaret, *shaan* (*sahn*), *mehrab* (*mihrab*), and the prayer hall (with its skylight and floor light lines that indicate the direction of Mecca, as well as its flaring mushroom capital concrete columns)—has been rethought afresh. Most poignant is the steel and glass bridge—representing *Pul-e-Siraat (As-Sirat*), the bridge over which everyone must pass on the Day of Judgment before entering Paradise—that connects to the complex's east wing, which comprises the women's prayer hall (significantly, not hidden but given formal prominence to the street), living quarters for the imam and his family, and a naturally ventilated ablution space. This elevated bridge, forming one side of the *shaan*, frames a perfect view of the verdant Azimpur cemetery. It is a beautiful moment of contemplation, one of life and the hereafter in a single frame. It is also a highly charged urban space—a physical nexus between the cacophony of urban chaos and the vast stillness of a city of graves.

Another building loaded with symbolism, but in this case associated with the formation of Bangladesh's national identity and independence movement, is the square and associated buildings named after Bangabandhu Sheikh Mujibur Rahman (1920–1975), the politician, revolutionary, statesman, and activist, commonly referred to as the "Father of the Nation." The location is Talaimari Chattar in Rajshahi, a town west of Dhaka, known for its silk and as the country's "City of Education." The project (2018–) is close to the Padma River and occupies the once-dusty site of a former truck interchange. Located on a busy intersection, its public-facing, curving plan form follows the street line. A series of brick-clad boxes forms a massive acoustic wall that conceals the "square": a quiet, introspective series of contained spaces, steps, pools, greenery, and elevated courtyards. The building becomes a water collector and a people collector. Azam's intention here is not to glorify the man—

Bangabandhu—with a commemorative monument, but instead provide a place for gathering and community education. Inside will be meeting, museum, and gallery spaces. Yet the bulk of the accommodation is given over to shared open public spaces: places to sit, gardens to seek shade, places of retreat. At night, the lighting of the staggered box forms transforms the complex into an urban landmark, its profile monumental, its elevated rain trees silhouetted against the night sky. A project like this sees Azam again focus on city building, using a relatively modest-scaled structure to at once repair a down-at-heel section of the city and act as a new surgical implant, completely reimagining what constitutes the public realm in a typical Bangladeshi urban context.

In a completely different setting, on an unusual greenfield site and with no urban context to use as a guiding parameter, Azam created a completely new landscape setting for the Sheikh Kamal IT Training and Incubation Centre at Narail, southwest of Dhaka en route to Jessore. A seven-story linear slab has been designed as a giant, partially hollowed-out brick screen, with a mix of angled and orthogonally aligned floor-to-ceiling brick baffle walls. On one side of the building, a series of baffles are highlighted as exposed off-form concrete, perforated with tiny holes like old-fashioned computer punch cards. The same treatment is applied to the exposed off-form concrete escape stairs that cantilever dramatically from the building's sculptural prow. This end of the building is treated like a giant artwork. Steel frames fashioned like computer circuit boards hang from the horizontal beams of a huge pergola that is itself supported off tall brick piers that emerge from a water-lily-studded lake. At the same time, one could also read this composition as if Azam has created a huge architectural tree emerging from the lake, which then transforms into the artwork, and into a more conventional yet sophisticated office/education building structure. Designed as a prototype for an envisaged fourteen more such schools, this building suggests a new direction for Azam—a move into institutional buildings for education. The project also sits within part of a larger, government-led national narrative about Bangladesh's wish to foster a new generation of young professionals skilled in information technology, continuing the legacy of high-quality tertiary education in sciences and engineering that in earlier times produced an internationally significant figure like structural engineer Fazlur Khan (1929–1982).[7]

What this project also points to is the need for a larger conversation about architecture in Bangladesh more generally. From the outside, and especially from a non-Western perspective, the country is often seen in architectural terms in just two ways. The first is from the standpoint of the legacy of the years of decolonization, of architect pioneers like Muzharul Islam following in the deep footsteps of Louis Kahn and other Americans like Daniel C. Dunham and Robert Boughey.[8] This history is rich with international connections and highlights the contested forms of modernism and their association with emergent nationalism across the Indian sub-continent and Southeast Asia. It deserves and has duly received expert documentation.[9] The second preconception from outside is from the standpoint of how to respond to questions of abject poverty in a country like Bangladesh. This is a real and pressing issue and needs to be addressed—as it does across many parts of the so-called Third World. But on another level,

Faculty of Fine Arts, University of Dhaka, designed by renowned Bangladeshi architect Muzharul Islam.

this second preconception is also a cliched view from the outside. On the one hand, it has given rise to important humanitarian works and publications on those works over the past twenty years.[10] But on the other hand, it has often led to the idea that this is the only problem or challenge facing architecture in Bangladesh. The question of what lies between—in a country like Bangladesh—in the yawning gaps where so-called "progress" might be found in terms of urbanization and urban design applicable to every social class and the architecture of housing, education, and governance for an emergent and aspirant lower, middle, and upper class, is often overlooked. Rafiq Azam's contributions, for example, to the development and typological variety of high-density residential design in dense, tropical urban settings are remarkable and deserve greater international recognition. But the myopic view of what constitutes Bangladeshi modern architecture often obscures the reality of local innovation, hard-won expertise in material practices, and formidable architectural and programmatic dexterity.

All the more significant then are Azam's buildings outside Bangladesh. They speak not just of Azam's expanded horizon, but also as representations of Bangladesh and its current crop of prodigious architectural talent. One of his earliest buildings outside Bangladesh was the SP Setia Headquarters Building (2014) in Shah Alam, a satellite city at the edge of Kuala Lumpur. There, in the design of an eight-story corporate office complex, Azam stamped his "green" credentials with the first private commercial building in Malaysia to receive a Platinum Certification for "green architecture." It was achieved with elements that Azam had brought from "home": a floating off-form concrete parasol roof, punctuated with his signature circle cutouts, impossibly tall concrete columns like tree trunks, and a water body with "floating" islands of garden. This is a building about rain and rainwater harvesting, green roofs and double glazing, and smart shading details. It's also about Bangladesh, especially Dhaka, interpreted architecturally by Azam and transported across the region to a new tropical context—and it works.

Perhaps in no other project is that sense of transposing architectural ideals intrinsic to Dhaka, and by extension Bangladesh, to other places more visible than in the two embassy buildings designed by Azam, one for neighboring Bhutan (2010–2025), the other for Pakistan (2007–2025). In Bhutan, this is subtle. The material and formal choices selected for the chancery and ambassador's residence in Thimphu in Bhutan are required, by royal decree, to conform closely to that country's strict architectural precepts and traditions: base walls of local Himalayan stone, projecting timber window bays (both *payab* and *rabsel* window types), timber bracketed eaves, low-pitched hip roofs, and main walls of rammed earth.[11] But what Azam brings is his constant design thematics: the all-encompassing parasol; a vast framed view of a distant landscape (the Himalayas) with a flat expanse of water (the Bay of Bengal) at your feet. A bust of Bangabandhu hovers above the water. As always, Azam uses architecture as framing elements for the larger story of landscape, both distant and immediate.

At the Bangladesh Chancery Complex in Islamabad (2007–2025), Azam returns again to red brick, the venerable age-old material common to both countries' deep archaeological pasts, both centered around two great river-based civilizations of the past, the Indus Valley and the

The Sears Tower under construction, circa 1973

world's largest delta formed by the Ganges, Padma, and Meghna rivers. Behind the obligatory high-security wall (now common to all embassies worldwide), an architectural "landscape" of brick is created, one of steps, walls, paved and grassed terraces, and block-like red-brick forms. Azam introduces another tall concrete parasol: its roof is perforated with giant circular openings of different diameters—a horizontal *jali* held aloft and supported off tall columns that sit in a pool of water. Paved in black, the pool's surface becomes a shimmering mirror, dappled circles dancing on its surface. The parasol above is long, oversailing, and covers the chancery at one end and the ambassador's residence at the other. It is the scheme's unifying element. A wing of staff accommodation leads off at right angles. Behind and surrounding the sides of the complex is a densely planted forest. The Bangladeshi flag—its red disk on a green background—stands tall in the forecourt entry. The red signifies the blood of those who fought and died for the nation's independence in 1971. The green represents the nation's lush landscape. In Azam's work, the circle appears often and almost always in the context of landscape, trees, and water. It is as if with this motif, he suggests a fundamental connection with the elements of sun, shadow, sky, and ground—but also, though never stated, a fiercely proud connection with the country that is Bangladesh.

Over the past decade, the work of Rafiq Azam has broadened its intellectual, spatial, and experiential repertoire. It has also crossed national and geographic borders. Apart from the brace of multinational firms whose work largely confers global branding (often without significant effect), few architects in the region have done this, especially those who were born there. One example might be Indonesian architect Kamil Ridwan, whose firm Urbane has designed important projects in Indonesia, Singapore, India, and China. But Ridwan's personal trajectory has shifted more to politics, as the current governor of West Java. Rafiq Azam, by contrast, has chosen to remain faithful to his calling in designing architecture and landscapes, and in remaining true to the place of his birth, Old Dhaka. This is a virtuous and, it has to be said, a long game. All of the projects illustrated in this book evidence that long-held commitment. However, what has become emphasized, perhaps more than ever before in the works of the last decade, is his commitment to the common good (*al-maslaha al-'amma*)[12] as expressed through architecture and its engagement with that most public place, the city. Ten years ago, Azam spoke to me of trying to provide everyone with an opportunity to find their "personal forest," their "personal lake," or a place to find peace.[13] That search has not ended, it has simply been extended and upscaled: his horizon has expanded.

Azimpur, Dhaka, 2022

[1] Oscar Riera Ojeda (ed), *Kerry Hill: Crafting Modernism* (Thames & Hudson, 2013).
[2] Philip Goad, "A New Third World Modernism: Critical Design Strategies in the Architecture of Rafiq Azam," in Rosa Maria Falvo (ed.), *Rafiq Azam: Architecture for Green Living* (Skira Editore, 2013), pp. 37–45. In this essay, I explain "dreaming," "finding," and "making Dhaka" as strategies critical to Azam's design practice.
[3] Azam visited Japan in 2004. While there he visited and studied the work of Tadao Ando in and around Osaka. He also contacted Toshiroh Ikegami, Ando's ex-partner of five years, to learn specifically about off-form concrete construction techniques employed by the Ando office. On that same trip in 2004, Azam attended the Glenn Murcutt master class at the Arthur and Yvonne Boyd Education Centre at Shoalhaven in NSW, Australia.
[4] See, for example, public commentary on concrete, construction, and sustainability in Jonathan Watts, "Concrete: the most destructive material on Earth," *The Guardian* (February 25, 2019): https://www.theguardian.com/cities/2019/feb/25/concrete-the-most-destructive-material-on-earth
[5] See David Harvey, "The Right to the City," *International Journal of Urban and Regional Research*, 27: 4 (2003), pp. 939–941. For expanded versions, see David Harvey, "The Right to the City," *New Left Review*, 53 (September/October 2008) and David Harvey, *Rebel Cities: From the Right to the City to the Urban Revolution* (Verso, 2012).
[6] Liane Lefaivre, Ingeborg de Roode et.al (eds.), *Aldo van Eyck: The Playgrounds and the City* (Stedelijk Museum, 2002).
[7] Fazlur Rahman Khan was a world-famous structural engineer, born and initially trained in Bangladesh. He was responsible for leading innovations in twentieth-century skyscraper design, especially in the United States. He became a partner in the Chicago office of Skidmore, Owings & Merrill and was responsible for the structural design of hundreds of tall buildings, including in Chicago the one hundred-story John Hancock Center (1965–1969) and the Sears Tower (1970–1974), the tallest building in the world from 1973 to 1998. See Yasmin Sabina Khan, *Engineering Architecture: The Vision of Fazlur R. Khan* (WW Norton, 2004).
[8] See, for example, Martino Stierli, Anoma Pieris, and Sean Anderson (eds), *The Project of Independence: Architectures of Decolonization in South Asia, 1947–1985* (Museum of Modern Art, 2022).
[9] Significant books that cover these histories include: Kazi Khaleed Ashraf and James Belluardo (eds.), *An Architecture of Independence: The Making of South Asia* (Architectural League of New York, 1998); Peter Scriver and Vikramaditya Prakash, *Colonial Modernities: Building, Dwelling and Architecture in British Ceylon* (Routledge, 2007); Duanfang Lu (ed.), *Third World Modernism: Architecture, Development and Identity* (Routledge, 2011); and Anoma Pieris, *Architecture and Nationalism in Sri Lanka: The Trouser Under the Cloth* (Routledge, 2013).
[10] Recent publications on humanitarian architecture are numerous. Important publications including those by editors of Architecture for Humanity: *Design Like You Give a Damn: Architectural Responses to Humanitarian Crises* (Metropolis Books, 2006); Marie J. Aquilino (ed.), *Beyond Shelter: Architecture for Crisis* (Thames & Hudson, 2011); and Alice Min Soo Chun and Irene E Brisson (eds.), *Grounds Rules for Humanitarian Design* (Wiley West, 2015). The recent survey of contemporary Bangladesh architecture, Andreas Ruby (ed.), *Bengal Stream: The Vibrant Architecture Scene of Bangladesh* (Christoph Merian Verlag, 2017), also has extensive coverage of humanitarian architecture.
[11] *Bhutanese Architecture Guidelines* (The Ministry of Works and Human Settlement, Royal Government of Bhutan, Thimphu, 2014): https://www.moit.gov.bt/wp-content/uploads/2010/11/Bhutan-Arch-Guidelines-final-2014.pdf.
[12] Dale F. Eickelman and Armando Salvatore, "Public Islam and the common good," *Etnográfica*, 10: 1, 2006, pp. 97–105.
[13] Interview with Rafiq Azam, Dhaka, February 14, 2013.

tropical antiquity

SP SETIA HEADQUARTERS

Shah Alam, Malaysia

2012–2014

SP Setia is one of the largest property developers in Malaysia. In the conceptual phase of this large office project, the Persiaran Setia, a major highway to the south of the city and a large rainwater reservoir on the east side were significant in determining the planning and design decisions. To facilitate public connectivity and visibility from a distance, this southeast corner was developed with particular care. The avoidance of any typical boundary demarcations on the east flank, together with physical and visual links with the rainwater catchment pond and the surrounding landscape, endow this building with a certain humility, without forgoing the importance of its urban identity. Nine monumental columns rising up 36.58 meters support and project its large, cantilevered parasol into the sky. The introduction of a large, shallow water body at ground level harvests the frequent rain and protects the building in a fire emergency while paying homage to the tropical conditions in this region. This project was conceived according to state-of-the-art "green construction" standards and is the first private commercial building in Malaysia to receive the platinum certification for green architecture.

The façades facing north, east, and south comprise double-glazing curtain walls with full-height low-E glass to allow optimal daylight penetration with minimal solar heat gain and glare. The west-facing façade is in reinforced concrete with few openings. Building services are located on the western façade, reducing reliance on mechanical cooling. The tower rooftops and annex building are covered with turf and landscaped to help minimize solar heat gain and the cooling load requirement. The use of sustainable materials was emphasized throughout the building and a rainwater harvesting system facilitates the wastewater and irrigation infrastructures. General open-plan workstations with one-meter-high clear glass panel partitions allow unobstructed views across the open space, with external views shared by all, and also help cut down the need for artificial lighting.

CHI SEAFOOD
Setia

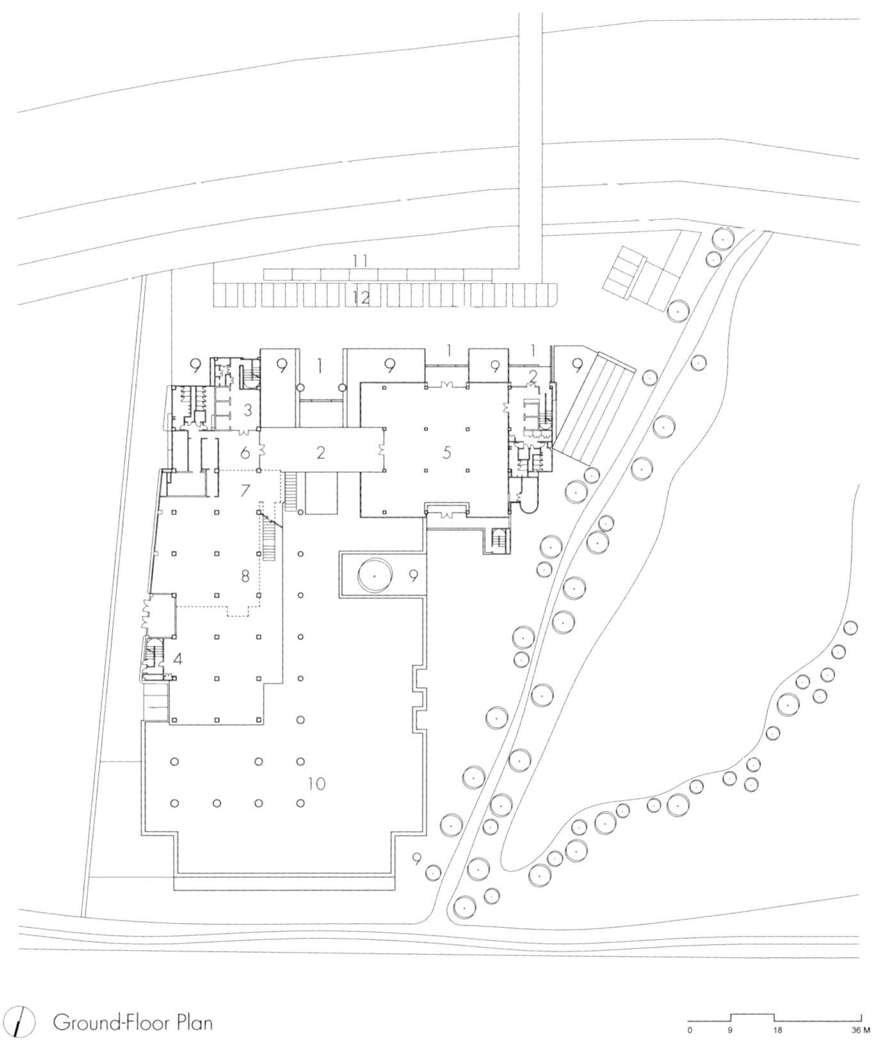

1. porch
2. foyer
3. lobby
4. staircase
5. commercial block
6. reception
7. waiting lounge
8. gallery space
9. garden area
10. water body
11. bus parking
12. car parking

previous page
View from Setia Persiaran Highway in Shah Alam, Selangor, Malyasia.

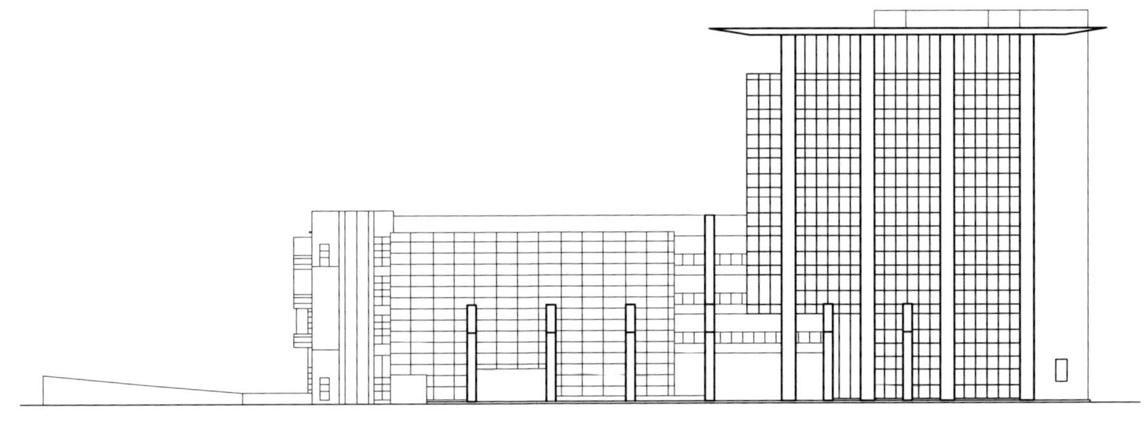

South Elevation

Sunlight through the oculus in the water court.

previous page
Water court on the top floor.

Northern entrance.

View from the water catchment lawn.

sacred diplomacy

EMBASSY OF THE PEOPLE'S REPUBLIC OF BANGLADESH
THIMPHU BHUTAN

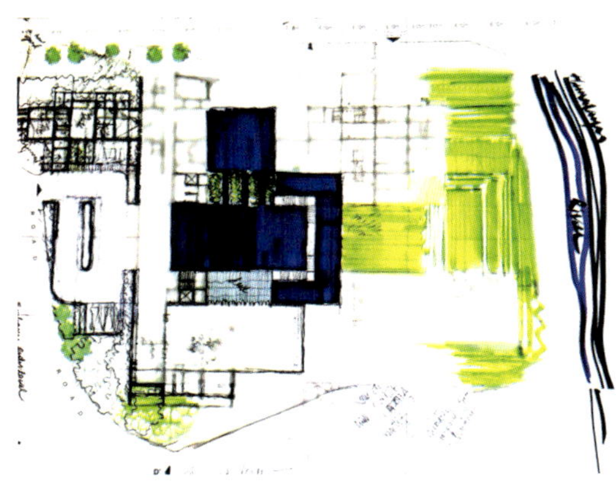

BANGLADESH CHANCERY COMPLEX

Thimphu, Bhutan
2010–2025

On December 6, 1971, Bhutan became the first country to send a telegram recognizing Bangladesh's independence. King Jigme Dorji Wangchuck personally expressed support for Bangladesh's struggle and believed in its eventual success. This Bangladesh Chancery Complex and Ambassador's Residence in Thimphu embodies the harmonious fusion of the Bhutanese and Bangladeshi cultures, celebrating the historical and geographical connections between the two nations.

Four main themes were considered in this design development. First and foremost is the mutual primordial relationship with the precious water that flows from the Himalayas into the Bay of Bengal. The intention was to pay homage to this great mountain range by creating a water court symbolizing the bay at the foothills. Secondly, as per historical evidence, Bhutan recognized Bangladesh as the primary nation that actively participated in the reformation and propagation of Buddhism through the Buddhist saint Atish Dipankar. Thirdly, the climatic conditions of this site, with its mild summers and cold winters, were also an interesting opportunity to combine the two cultural realities. By utilizing the generous inclination of the sun, during the winter, a greenhouse effect was created that subsidizes heating costs. Bhutan strictly adheres to specific local regulations for its architectural expressions. Though there was a special waiver for this chancery complex design, the aim was to respectfully interpret the surrounding context through a close study of Bhutanese spaces and cultural narratives and elements.

1. formal entrance
2. water body
3. visa wing
4. hall and gallery
5. multipurpose hall
6. reception and lounge areas
7. visa wing
8. office
9. car drop off area
10. formal living room
11. dining room
12. kitchen
13. deck
14. parking area

page 170
Simtokha Dzong, Thimphu, Bhutan, 2024
Meaning "Palace of the Profound Meaning of Secret Mantras," it was built in 1628 and is an important historical monument and former Buddhist monastery.
Image courtesy of Zannat Jui

next page
Central water court representing the Bay of Bengal with the Himalayas blending in at the entrance level.

Central water court
(under construction).

Social window at
the entrace level
(under construction).

next page
Social window at the entrance with a view of the central water court.

old Dhaka-new story

CONVERSATION
ROSA MARIA FALVO & RAFIQ AZAM

part two

RMF

The origins of the Mughal city of "Puran Dhaka," otherwise referred to as Old Dhaka, are over four centuries old and reportedly as fluid and majestic as the rivers surrounding it. This area has witnessed the rise and fall of empires, changing cultures, and the evolution of a new nation. Traditions are still alive in its vibrant districts—Lalbagh, Hazaribagh, Chowkbazar, Bangsal, Gendaria, Kotwali, Wari, and Sutrapur. What was it like to grow up there?

RA

It was exciting. There was always something on and we spent our childhood weaving through its labyrinthine streets. I have very fond memories of belonging there. It's still overflowing with life and neighbors still know each other, something that hardly exists in the newer parts of Dhaka, like Gulshan and Baridhara. Colorful rickshaws constantly compete, tea shops are always full, and kids play cricket wherever they can swing a bat. There are something like three thousand or so heritage buildings in Old Dhaka that have fallen into disrepair, but it still holds its charm and endless stories. We have to continue raising awareness to restore these areas before our cultural history disappears.

I graduated in 1989, not very long after our country was both devasted and transformed by the Liberation War. This nation has been enriched by so many philosophies and influences, but unfortunately, very few buildings remain to remind us of its grand past. Those still standing, like the archaeological relics of Wari-Bateshwar, Paharpur, Mahasthangarh, Lalmai-Mainamati, and other architectural jewels like the Kantajew Temple, Shat Gambuj Mosque, Lalbagh Fort, and Curzon Hall, still testify to the wealth of Bangladesh's cultural and architectural history.

Lalbagh Fort, Old Dhaka, 2010
Imagery on pp. 183–189,
courtesy of Rosa Maria Falvo

RMF

Bengali architecture fuses indigenous elements of the Subcontinent with influences from other parts of the world—it's an amalgamation of ancient urban, religious, and rural vernacular styles, colonial townhouses and modern ones. I've heard it described as the architecture of "wind, water, and clay." I was fortunate to see the Somapura Mahavihara, constructed by the Pala rulers and now UNESCO World Heritage, with its decorative clay bricks from the ancient Bengal Delta.

RA

Yes, it beautifully demonstrates our heritage, with its square platforms and burnt-brick panels featuring geometric patterns and sculptural compositions. The Aga Khan Academy, which we worked on in collaboration with Feilden Clegg Bradley Studios in London, is our largest educational project to date and the design was inspired by this Buddhist learning center, emphasizing shared spaces—like sanctuaries—attached to living and working quarters. Various brick buildings simulate the traditional open layout and courtyards, so that students today can freely move, play, and chat freely. Using mainly locally sourced bricks and brickwork traditions, the whole place expresses a layering of artistry that's based on the intellectual, physical, spiritual, and moral development ideals of these original Buddhist universities that once existed in Bangladesh. The landscaping is also sculpted and heavily planted on all four sides of the central *maidan* (square), which is the social heart of the school that aims to nurture a sense of belonging, tranquility, and communal harmony.

Somapura Mahavihara archaeological site, Paharpur, Bangladesh, 2009

RMF

By contrast, the absurdities of Dhaka's inner "concrete jungle" are evident even to first-time visitors. It encompasses such different kinds of worlds, full of stark contrasts. There are still misconceptions about it, as the world looks on from afar. How can we better understand your local realities?

RA

I think there's definitely miscommunication or a lack of understanding about Dhaka. Academically speaking, the concept of a "functioning" city based on European standards, of population density for instance, simply doesn't apply when you see numbers here that are almost unintelligible. So you have to reconsider your whole definition of what a city actually is or can be. For example, the people living in Shahidnagar, at the southwestern end of Old Dhaka on the shores of the Buriganga River, have long been in one of the world's most densely populated areas, with more than a staggering 168,000 people per square kilometer. And the numbers increase all the time. But despite traffic standstills and very poor amenities, this low-income community continues its unusually strong social bonding. You can see this city's beating heart in its trafficked waterways. People are constantly migrating from rural areas looking for work and many end up in slums. There's a lot of pressure to build up and modernize the already overburdened infrastructure. Shoddily constructed buildings pop up quickly and are the first to collapse in a serious earthquake.

RMF

Dhaka certainly defies logic and tests your optimism and tolerance.

RA

Yes, it's full of extremes and contradictions: there's great affluence and great poverty, adaptive genius and resourcefulness, total ineptitude and dysfunction, enormous daily sacrifice and outrageous corruption—it's all here. You might say that about any big city, but this one is archetypal. All you have to do is sit in the back of a rickshaw or even a private car to experience its frustrations and relentless energy—it truly never stops! But I believe now is the time to create something that's different, beyond these old struggles and standards. Dhaka now holds possibilities.

RMF

Climate change is clearly threatening low-lying cities like this one. Bangladesh is often cited as the ultimate litmus test and Dhaka's experiences might be equally applied elsewhere. What is your outlook?

RA

Despite, and actually because of, its vulnerabilities, Bangladesh has had to establish some good examples of adaptation to climate change. There are early warning systems for floods and cyclones, as well as a vast network of shelters, that have saved countless lives and shown that effective planning is feasible even with limited resources. There are nature-based solutions, like planting trees on major highways, like on the Dhaka-Chattogram Road, which help protect infrastructure, biodiversity, and contribute to better air quality. So it's not all gloom, but I'm very interested to see what the young architects of the world are focused on, and how they will act to repair the damage and rebalance the disparities.

RMF
You've described your attraction to working in Old Dhaka as a way of "coming home." What do you mean by that?

RA
Old Dhaka has mercilessly fallen into mayhem in the absence of visionary planning. Increasing migration in an already overpopulated city has added to these difficulties. The amount of green and accessible open spaces is diminishing. So to address this urban crisis, the DSCC authorities took an ambitious step back in 2016 to revitalize the parks and playgrounds in Old Dhaka through a major initiative called *Jol Shobuje Dhaka* ("Dhaka as aqueous green").

RMF
Your Mayor Mohammad Hanif Jame Mosque project at the edge of the Azimpur graveyard in Old Dhaka is a case in point. I found this place to be spiritually moving, regardless of one's religious background. I think it really bridges the collective fervor of the streets with the private ritual of prayer.

RA
Yes, this burial ground is over two centuries old and it's an emotional space for me. In 2015, I was invited by the newly elected mayor to think about what could be done for Old Dhaka. After a long discussion, we arrived at the idea of a mosque and I was offered a modest fee, being the only source tender for this project. I discussed the idea with my mother, who told me it was an opportunity to serve the people of my birthplace, to pay homage to my father who rests there, and to create a place of gathering for good intentions. Inspired by her wisdom, I agreed to design it. My mother died in January 2016 and lies in the same graveyard.

The aim was to forge a practical bond between the city and its people, and the mosque was constructed almost entirely out of locally sourced bricks, sitting on 1,608 m^2 of land that belongs to the Dhaka South City Corporation. One of the key design features is the traditional *shaan*, an extended terrace at the entrance functioning as a kind of threshold. Philosophically, it's a symbolic confluence between the terrestrial city (past and present) and the celestial realm. The bridge to the north, inspired by the *Pul-e-Siraat* (bridge) mentioned in the Surah Maryam from the Qur'an, runs parallel to the graveyard and connects the upper levels of the main building, forming a frame of glass and steel to the graveyard beyond. I believe this project to be a beacon of hope for the future of our old city. It's an example of how architecture can navigate hegemony and corruption to create something meaningful for all concerned.

Kantajew Temple, Dinajpur, Bangladesh, 2009

RMF
Reviving the Rasulbagh Shishu Park has also been a milestone for you.

RA
Yes, that was one of my biggest challenges and great professional satisfactions. About two-hundred years ago, that whole area was a family graveyard owned by ink traders. It was left abandoned and people fought for its ownership. In 1984, these conflicts became violent and authorities intervened, opening a park in its place, but it was a band-aid fix that eventually failed because of neglect, and it was colonized by vagrants and criminals. The area was isolated and had no direct access to any main roads. Surrounded by residential buildings on all sides, with meter-wide alleys between them, the only entry points were at the southwest corner and along the northern wall, with the only adjacent road congested with makeshift shops and tea shops that further hampered access. During the rainy seasons, the narrow alleys would regularly flood due to a lack of proper drainage. The rainwater also mixed with overflowing sewage from the open drains, making it all very unsanitary. The area was derelict and plagued by social conflict. Within the park, the grass had withered away, the walls were crumbling and covered in graffiti, and the trees were malnourished. There was an abandoned three-story veterinary clinic on the western side and an active mosque in the southeast corner. Locals had to walk through the park to access the mosque and would frequently use the open field for rituals and religious activities when the interior was full. Since there were no proper walkways or ground covers and damaged seating, many people, including children and the elderly, had to pray on the bare ground. An old Banyan tree—the type under which Bangladeshis traditionally celebrate festivals and mourn their deceased—was located in the northwest corner and was still used regularly. And despite being named a "Shishu Park" (children's park) it had no games or sporting facilities and was not even a safe location for families. Fortunately, the locals were actively involved in trying to prevent its misuse, but their limited resources restricted what they could do. So we took on the challenge to transform the whole place.

Negotiating with local politicians and bureaucrats was hard work, as they were entrenched in maintaining the status quo. It was necessary to guide them very closely so they could finally see it was in their interests to regain the community's trust by delivering effective outcomes, within the budget. The selection of capable and honest construction workers was also part of this delicate political rehabilitation process.

Public involvement and consensus, with lots of debates, was absolutely crucial to the long-term success of such a symbiotic relationship. We had to tear down the barriers, physically and symbolically. Basically, the first stage was focused on engaging the various community stakeholders to set the direction of the work so that at the end of the process they would own the responsibility of maintenance and upkeep. In the second stage, the goal was to renew the entire area based on their needs and desires, focusing on accessibility, functionality, and aesthetics. We led meetings with many of the community's elders, imams (senior figures in the mosque), and local youth to get their feedback before holding a public hearing in the park.

Once the design was finalized and approved, the renovations began with the construction of the rainwater-harvesting trench and the removal of the north boundary wall. The adjacent road was incorporated into the park and remade into a promenade directly accessible by all. We built new drainage and piping systems to collect excess rainwater and runoff from the surface simultaneously. The new promenade was constructed at a half-meter elevation to allow for the new drainage system—a temporary sewage hold—that controls the flow and slowly expels it through a narrow drain. The rainwater-collection trenches also act as aqueducts that divert rainwater away from sewage ducts and carry it into a new filtration system.

The previously abandoned veterinary clinic was renovated and repurposed as a multifunctional building. The ground floor contains the new water filtration system and a women's club. The upper floors contain a councilor's office, a library, and a gym, with a coffee shop on the rooftop and solar panels generating 1.2 kilowatts to cover half of the building's energy needs. The exterior of the mosque was also renovated and space for ablutions was added, with numerous other decorative ones around the park. We constructed a small amphitheater around the old Banyan tree to facilitate events and festivities and all the other pre-existing trees in the park were incorporated into the design. Almost no trees were cut down in the entire process. The planting includes Carissa Carandas, Averrhoa Bilimbi, and Burmese grapes fresh from the trees. Close to the old Banyan tree, there's a Dhaak tree with blazing red leaves and there are orchards along the edges of the park with Kalabati trees and other plants that soak up excess water during the rainy season. All the rainwater runs through the trench into a filtration system and is then distributed. A public tap yard located in the northwest corner of the park serves as the main distribution point for free drinking water. The park's new design emphasizes maintaining a healthy and clean environment, so waste and recycling bins are available to encourage that.

The park now also boasts a proper sports field and separate children's playground, a pavilion, a 155-meter walkway, a public plaza, an Eidgah, and public restrooms. It has become a truly welcoming and family-friendly space.

RMF
I don't think Western audiences realize the degree of difficulty you and your teams and professional colleagues have to deal with in Bangladesh. These initiatives for transforming areas are courageous and exceptional.

RA
If a challenge becomes a problem, it's misery. But if you think of it as an opportunity for innovation, it can become a celebration. I aim to create social spaces where people can finally enjoy a sense of belonging. It's been so educational for me as well, creating small green oases that double as water-catchment areas. We have implemented many features to aid in the park's upkeep. Not all the water collected by the aqueducts is available to the public; stored rainwater is also used via the underground piping for irrigation, providing a hands-free approach to maintaining all the trees and greenery onsite. Public facilities including the café and library

Somapura Mahavihara archaeological site, Paharpur, Bangladesh, 2009

are a source of income and are managed by a local committee headed by the area's locally elected councilor. With around fifteen to twenty members, four of whom are from each of the four residential units with a direct line of sight to the park, this committee is the primary group for park management and is also responsible for hiring all the maintenance crew and organizing public events to promote community engagement. This puts the responsibility in the hands of those who value it most and strengthens the tight-knit relationships between local residents.

As an architect, the first thing I always contemplate is my role. It's been thirty years since I began my practice, and now I'm involved in my most ambitious projects yet—master planning for the southern half of Dhaka. So I can see how dramatically architecture can effect positive change for entire communities. Environmental factors not only impose constraints but also inspire creative thinking. To this end, Shatotto offers the Rafiq Azam Travel Bursary (RATB) to architecture students in India, Australia and Sri Lanka. This grant is rooted in the belief that they will benefit from experiencing our local realities to lead change in their own communities. In fact, most of the international award-winning projects from Bangladesh share a deep-rooted bond to our ancient values and knowledge while featuring innovations for climate, water, wind, soil, and material usage that are more than just sustainable. There's real interest here in urban design that directly improves people's daily lives.

RMF

I can't help but ask you about the turmoil that's happening at the moment. There are so many layers to social unrest as there are to social stability. Do you think it's delusional to presume that architecture can actually help save the world? Like the "New European Bauhaus" proposed by the EU in 2020, where architects, artists, students, engineers, designers, and scientists work together in a "cocreative space" to solve problems with climate change and urban living. What kind of responsibility do architects really have to develop this consciousness?

RA

Well, I believe we can positively influence each other to share different experiences, innovations, and creativity together. We have to work collaboratively and sensitively to improve our built environments. I don't see any other approaches to our problems or our ambitions that can make sense or bring about collective results. This kind of interdisciplinary thinking is much needed and amplifies international opportunities. For instance, I was honored to accept the challenge of designing the Bangladesh High Commission in Islamabad, Pakistan, and then also the Bangladesh Chancery Complex in Bhutan. In Pakistan, I realized we had to go beyond culture and climate, given our history, so the design needed to consider the very meaning of diplomacy and reconciliation, and navigate many conflicting emotions. My approach was to focus on our shared archaeological legacy, back to the time of the Indus Valley and Bengal civilizations, which was a kind of golden age for our two nations. The richness of these cultures would then form the foundations for creating new relationships today, in the hope of joining our potential to find solutions to climatic conditions. Similarly, for the Bhutan Embassy Complex, all sorts of friendly connections and historical referencing and

On the streets of Old Dhaka, 2010

interactions were used, from sharing Himalayan waters to our spiritual bonds, with Bhutan being the first country to recognize Bangladesh as an independent nation immediately after the Liberation War. All these elements were carefully considered as the foundations of our design criteria, and I used these projects to manage international relationships as part of my social responsibility as an architect.

RMF
Last year you had nothing short of a people's revolution!

RA
Yes, and it's quite extraordinary that you found yourself here in Dhaka during this unprecedented and tragically tumultuous time. The many wounds left behind are evident. This is actually very complicated, but architecture definitely has a significant role to play and it will take a lot of time and great commitment to make a difference. Everything is layered and these layers come together over time to create peace, or no peace. Everyone has a role. I was faced with many failing policies and a lack of understanding. The resources were there but they were being channeled elsewhere. The lack of accountability becomes another political problem and nothing happens. This is where architectural intervention and architects, supported by a mayor's good decision—a positive political stance—can suddenly make things come together. With experience, we learned the art of negotiation. I was born and raised in Old Dhaka, so I see that as my resource because I'm more intimately familiar with the issues on the ground. I have to be adamantly committed to not losing my temper. I can't be hell-bent on owning a project. So I see myself more as the catalyst, trying to facilitate, connect with the DSCC's powers to implement changes, and then mobilize various skilled actors to participate. If they don't know or trust each other, the whole thing becomes a social issue. So you must understand the whole context.

RMF
That's not like the stereotypical protagonist who performs with righteous confidence.

RA
I'm removing the protagonist from the scenario, although it's still a kind of performance, where you're listening and waiting for them to identify your idea and claim it as theirs, otherwise you can't implement it. We had to join the community, especially since I came from there, and I would remind them that my memories are still there. That's part of building trust.

MONTO TRADE
বিকাশ
করুন

চায়না
খেলনা
স্টোর

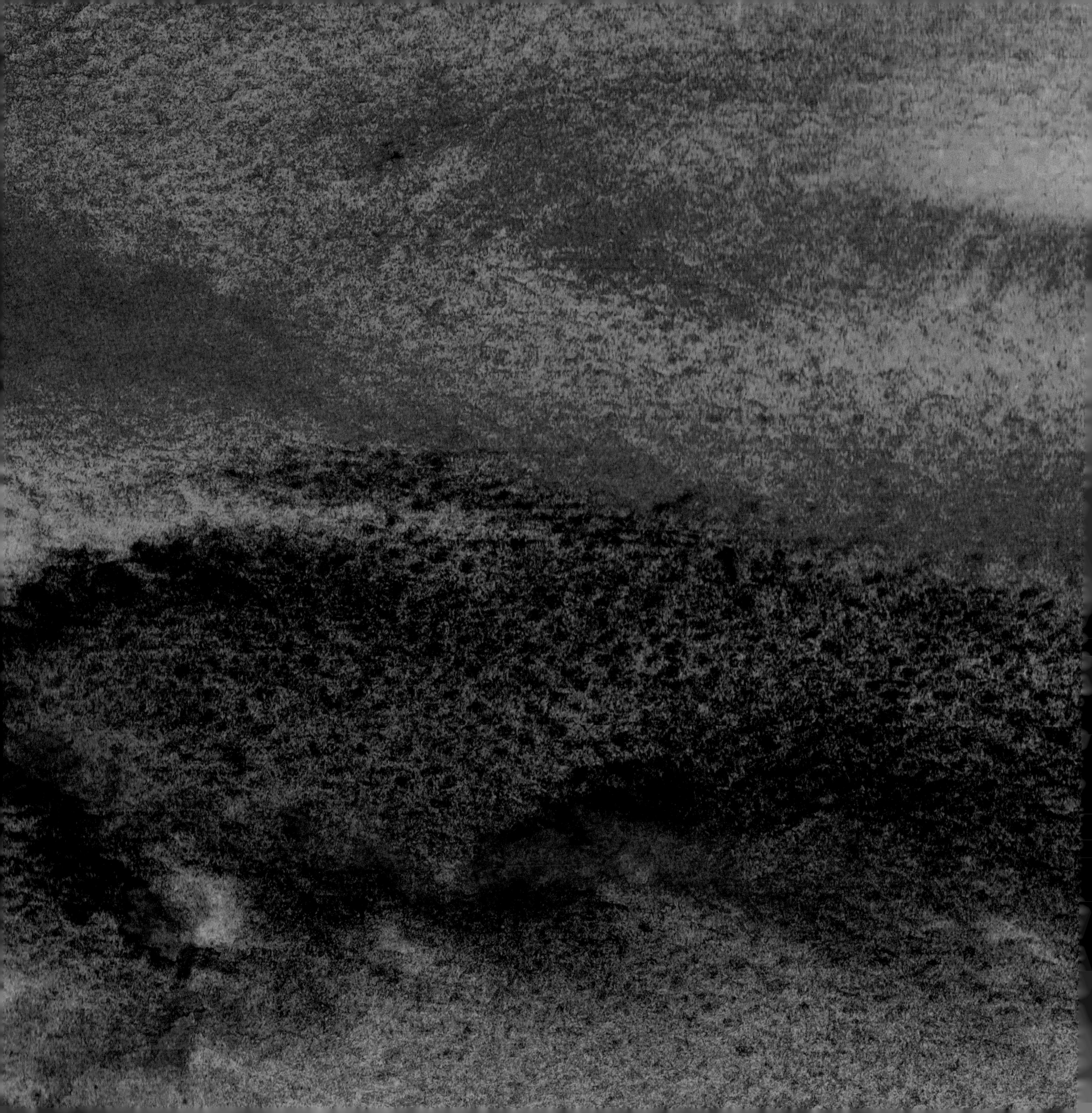

ethereal thresholds

মেয়র মোহাম্মদ হানিফ
জামে মসজিদ

MAYOR MOHAMMAD HANIF JAME MOSQUE

Azimpur, Dhaka

2016–2018

Located in Old Dhaka, adjacent to the Azimpur graveyard in Lalbagh, this historical area was established by the Mughals circa four hundred years ago. Mayor Mohammad Hanif Jame Mosque is situated on a 1500 m^2 plot that belongs to the Dhaka South City Corporation (DSCC). Much of this new design was inspired by two Mughal mosques in the Lalbagh area as departure points from traditional interpretations of mosque architecture. However, beyond its conceptual ideation, another challenge in this project was to educate and motivate the construction contractor who was obstructing its execution through corrupt political influence.

A key feature derived from Mughal mosques is the *sahn*, accommodating occasional religious gatherings and also acting as a social space for the regular devotees. Since this mosque borders Azimpur Road to the south and the community graveyard to the north, it acts as a threshold space between the terrestrial and celestial realms. This meticulous design incorporates structural convenience and spiritual aspiration. The main prayer hall on the western side of the plot is supported by mushroom-shaped columns that avoid beams and create a humble synergy between the existing trees in the adjacent graveyard. The prayer hall features a frosted-glass floor segment with a skylight that functions as the *mihrab* and is flanked by a brick *jali* on the south façade, which filters the street noise and simultaneously invites summer breezes and the sweet fragrance of jasmine that was specifically planted. On the north façade, the fenestrations are in clear glass to allow unobstructed views of the sky.

Traffic noise screening on the southern side.

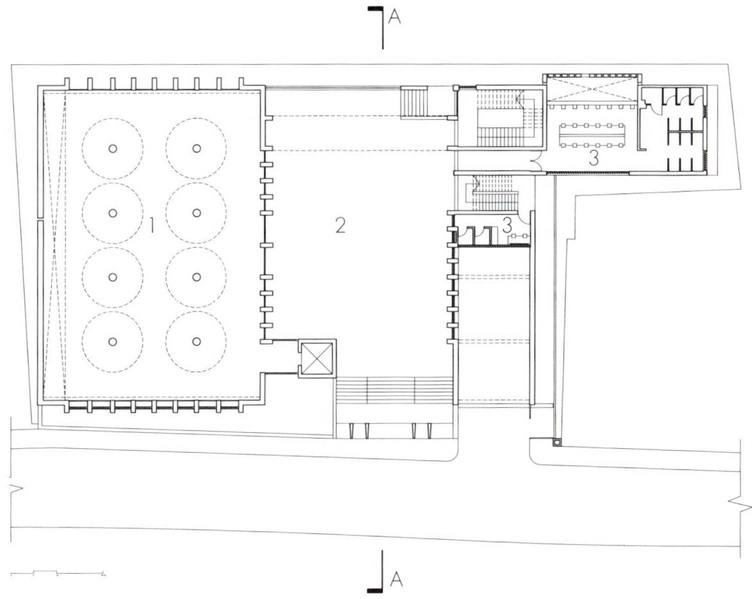

Ground-Floor Plan

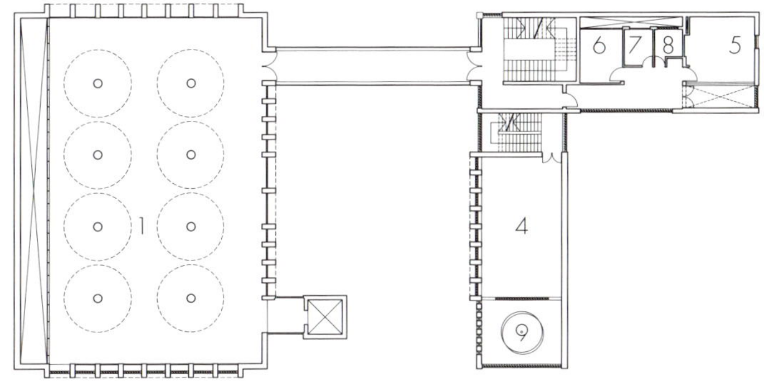

1st-Floor Plan

1. indoor prayer space
2. *shaan*
3. ablution space
4. prayer space for women
5. muezzin's room
6. imam's room
7. kitchenette
8. restroom
9. Bakul tree

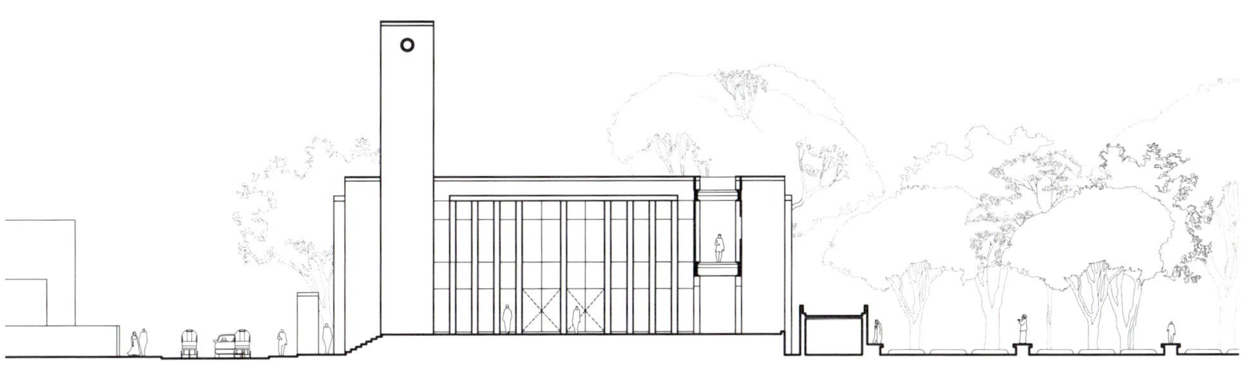

Section AA

previous page
Celestial light touching the *mehrab* attached to the *qibla* wall, indicating the direction of Mecca.

Women's prayer space.

Men's prayer space.

following pages
Shaan social space.

versatility

AZIMPUR PUBLIC RESTROOMS

Azimpur, Dhaka

2020–2023

The lack of public restrooms and the inadequacy of these facilities in the city of Dhaka demonstrates one of the most conspicuous urban planning failures over the last few decades. Local statistics suggest that people hardly use public toilets and women in particular avoid them due to their typically unsanitary conditions. This has led to widespread kidney problems across the population. This project called for a new approach to the design of public amenities and an overhaul of the entire existing area. Rather than simply building bathrooms, the idea here was to develop a three-story building on this 70 m^2 plot and incorporate the large existing rain tree, including a book shop, coffee shop with roof garden, and ground-floor restrooms. Due to the limited scale of this major, congested street corner, a composite structure of concrete and steel was employed to maximize the internal ground and floor areas. Because of the northern orientation of this building, glass was used unapologetically to allow unrestricted visibility throughout.

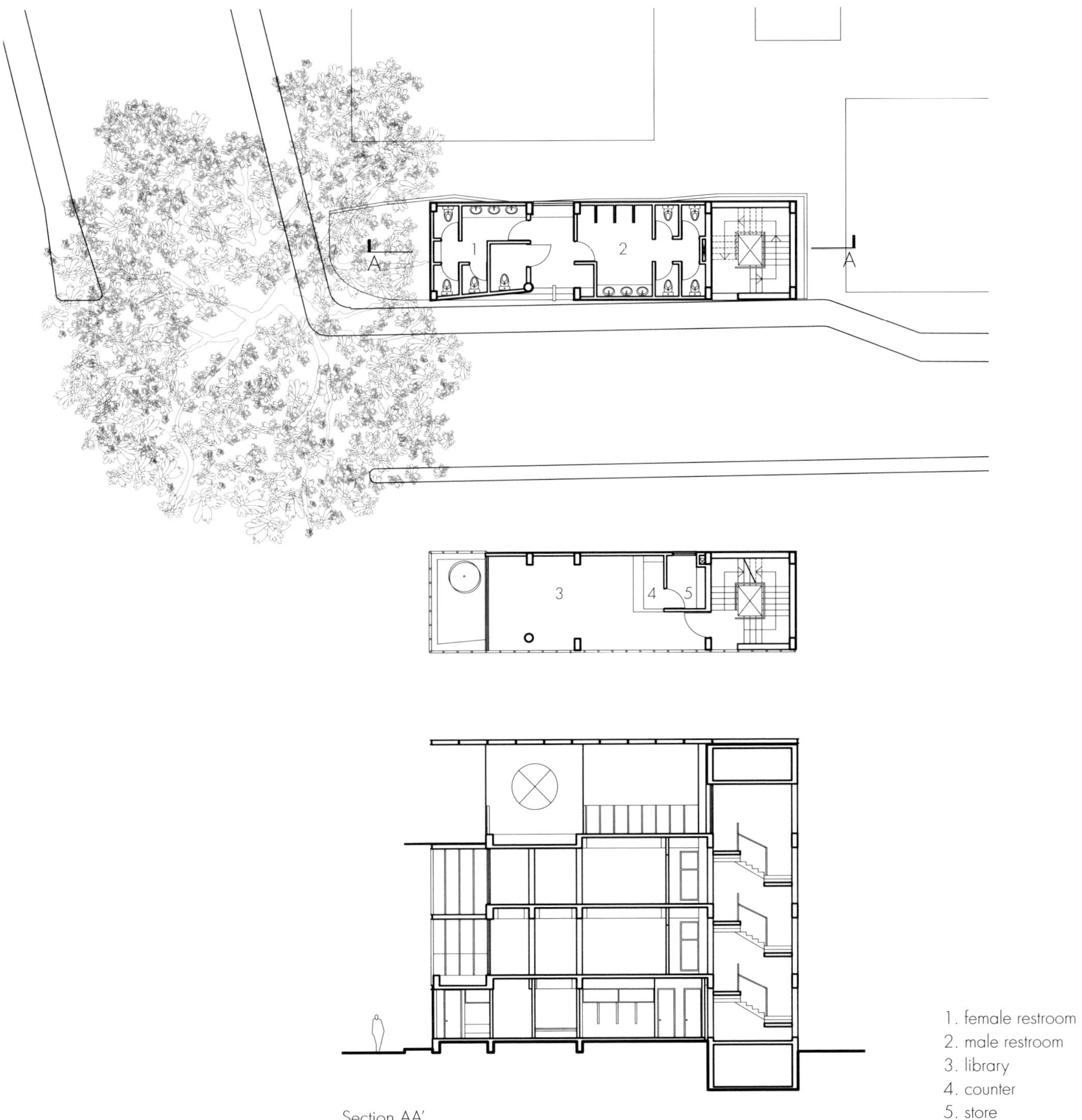

Section AA'

New public restrooms facility, with *Samanea saman* tree. Its leaves fold in rainy weather and in the evening, hence the name "rain tree."

পাবলিক টয়লে

PIZZA
12:00PM-04:00PM
OLD TOWN
minister
LED TV AC REFRIGERATOR
SSC

martyrs' ode

BAHADUR SHAH PARK

Johnson Road, Lalbagh, Dhaka
2017–2019

Located in the Laxmibazar area in Old Dhaka, this historical park commemorates the martyred sepoys who perished in the Indian Rebellion of 1857 against British colonial rule. The area harbors horrific memories for Bangladeshi citizens. During the failed "Sepoy Mutiny," some were mutilated by English soldiers of the British East India Company and others were hung on different trees for public display to instill fear among the commoners. It was also the venue from which the accession by Queen Victoria, former Queen of the British Empire and Empress of India, was announced amid much fanfare in 1858, when this area was named Victoria Park. In 1957, celebrating the centenary, the Dhaka Improvement Trust built a cenotaph designed by the celebrated architect Abdullah Thariani to commemorate the mutiny, and it was renamed Bahadur Shah Park after the last Mughal emperor, who was proclaimed leader of the mutiny.

When the park's revitalization began in 2016, it was evident that the nation's martyrs had been neglected and ignored. Illicit and antisocial activities were rife in the area, which was poorly managed and in a derelict state. During the design process, several simple and effective steps were taken to improve the park's accessibility. Surrounding fencing that had several unlicensed shops was dismantled and a more inclusive approach was proposed. Beautiful walkways, naturally shaded by the existing trees, were redesigned and a water management system was integrated for the entire premises. The primary design element here was the project's lighting, which now vividly illuminates the central cenotaph to honor the fallen.

1. existing monument
2. public gymnasium

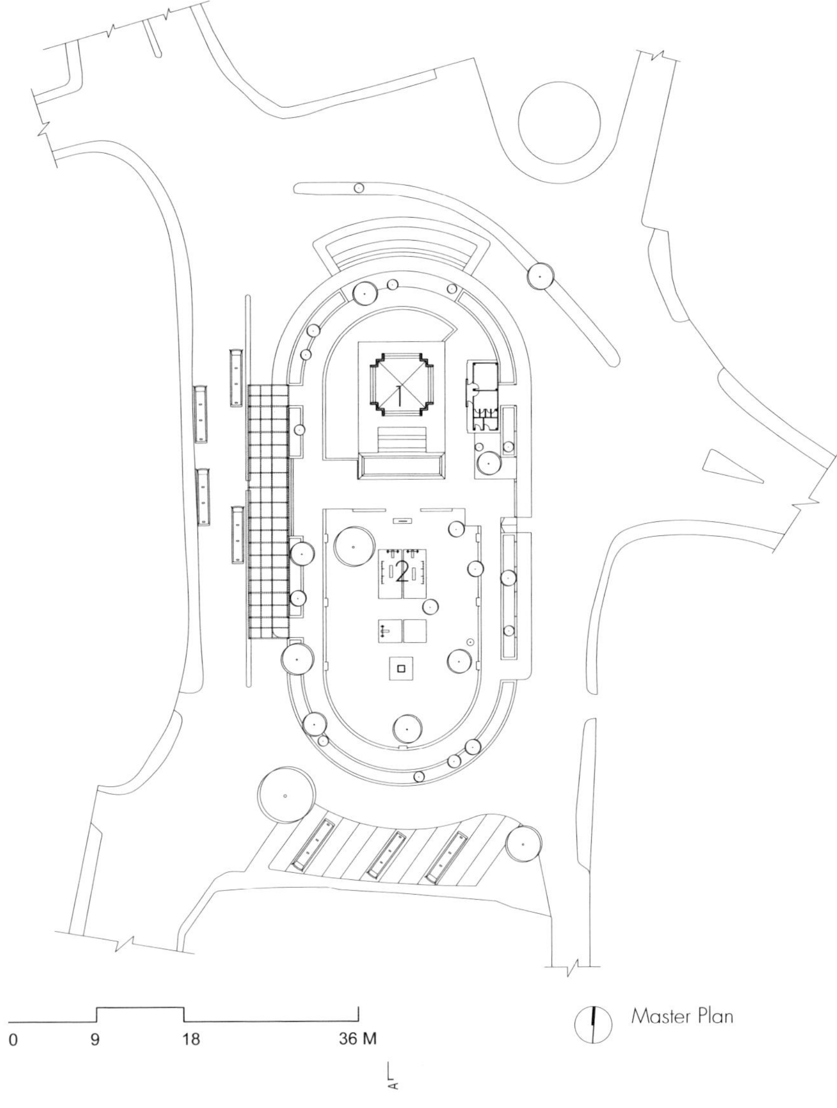

Master Plan

Section AA

top and bottom
Decrepit conditions before the renovation.

next page
New park boundaries and walkways after renovation.

next page
Renovated cenotaph dedicated to the martyred sepoys in the Sepoy Mutiny of 1857.

পাবলিক
টয়লেট

ARCHITECTURE OF INCLUSIVITY

GEORGE KUNIHIRO

private and public

Architecture is both public and private. It occupies a ground area and three-dimensional space, which upon realization becomes visible to those who can access the view. It becomes part of a collective context whether it stands in an urban setting or shares its existence with natural surroundings. Visibility ensures that an existing building has a public character at the very least. However, its function determines its true character. Possession of a building gives the owner the right to share the spatial experience with the public or to keep it in the private realm. The most private of typologies being residential architecture. The property on which it stands is open only to those permitted by the owner. Similarly, privately owned commercial and office buildings, hospitals, schools, and other institutional architecture have limited access. Only those belonging to tenants, members of an organization, and visitors are permitted by the stakeholders to have privileged access and use these buildings.

Public buildings, on the other hand, especially those that are owned by a municipality, or state or national government, belong to the collective of taxpayers, that is, they are commonly owned by the citizens of the respective jurisdictions. These stakeholders have their share of ownership to enjoy the convenience of public buildings such as government buildings, public libraries, museums, stadiums, and in some instances, public schools, hospitals, and even military facilities.

Rafiq Azam began his practice taking on residential clients for single-family homes, gradually moving up to design multifamily residential buildings. Mostly in the private sector, he was catering to upper-income households seeking comfort and luxury in their homes and in the communal areas of the building. Azam developed his own vocabulary utilizing clean orthogonal volumes, lush and colorful landscapes with water features, stepped terraces, dramatic atriums, framed vistas, and the remarkable flow of layered spaces. Having grown up in Dhaka's historic center, he is a proud citizen of this community and frequently returns to his origins, contributing to the improvement of the living conditions of its residents.

Bangladesh is an emerging economy, full of vitality, and has a national policy to continue its upward thrust, utilizing its youthful population as an energetic force for production operations in a wide spectrum of emerging industries. National policy to execute large urban redevelopment in this capital has seen local leadership commit to bringing Dhaka up to the same caliber of urban centers in other countries within the region. Although a historic city with a rich heritage, the chaos and dilapidation of its urban fabric and infrastructures over decades has resulted in serious traffic entanglements and countless illegally constructed buildings, affecting fire safety and public health. Crime rates have also risen and one typically sees private security personnel guarding the roadblocks in upper-income neighborhoods. Open spaces have been degraded to unmanaged vacant lots that have become meeting grounds for drug addicts and dealers. In order to transform these conditions, the municipality of Dhaka launched two major urban redevelopment plans over the past decade. This ambitious initiative aims to achieve a comprehensive realignment of traffic patterns, the installation of public transportation, and zoning innovation to remedy the overwhelming problems.

As a young boy, Azam's world was a densely populated residential neighborhood in Old Dhaka and its busy commercial life. The Buriganga River flows past its southwest outskirts and now ranks among the most polluted rivers in the country. In the twentieth century, the water table and river became polluted by polyethylene waste and other hazardous substances from demolished buildings near the riverbanks. By the time Rafiq was of school age, the family had moved to another part of the city. As a student of architecture at the Bangladesh University of Engineering and Technology (BUET), he recalls his poor performance and uncertainties about pursuing this career. But after joining an architectural office as a young apprentice, his original love of painting and drawing came to the fore. It helped him to remain in contact with the rich aquatic environment of his motherland, and after opening his own studio, his work began to be recognized with several awards abroad. Azam's masterfully poetic interpretations of hard edges and multilayered spaces, combined with his intuitive understanding of landscape, vegetation, and water bodies, became his design vocabulary with which to impact Dhaka's cityscape and other parts of Bangladesh, and beyond. Observing Azam's creative maneuvers, the late Syed Zaigham S. Jaffery, a respected senior Pakistani architect, gave Rafiq some advice: "One must continue his path forward to explore new horizons and not be satisfied with present success and accomplishments." This motivated Azam to reflect on his life as a boy, to frequently visit his grandmother in Old Dhaka, and to explore the deterioration of his original neighborhood. This journey back in time resulted in a new calling to immerse himself in the movement to transform the living conditions of his birthplace. In the past decade, his professional stature and practice have grown, and his work has gained international acclaim beyond the region to the global arena. His relationship with the local authorities came to fruition when he was appointed to draw up the master plan of the Dhaka South City Corporation. Typically, an experienced architectural practice that has achieved a certain size and portfolio of projects will continue to take on larger-scale ones to support the firm and showcase its capabilities. But Azam's primary motivation in taking on the enormous challenges of urban redevelopment comes from a uniquely personal epiphany as a "homeboy" of Old Dhaka. Precisely at this critical juncture of his career, he is looking back to repay his heritage and his experiences in this city. Azam has been working hard, against all external odds, to put forward a series of design proposals utilizing the functional innovations and artistic sensitivities of his talent. At the time of this publication, he had completed several public projects that have certainly become models for the larger redevelopment plan of the Dhaka South City Corporation. Azam has shifted his efforts from producing exclusive environments to ensuring an inclusive future for entire communities.

One such commission was to design the Mayor Mohammad Hanif Jame Mosque (2016–2018) in Old Dhaka. The site is located along an existing cemetery with a tree-covered graveyard, giving a rich natural backdrop to this sanctuary in the middle of the neighborhood. Its entrance courtyard is elevated from the busy street and the grand staircase leading worshippers of the Holy Quran becomes a public viewing stand and a place to gather along the sidewalk. The building projects its public character onto the street in a

Mayor Mohammad Hanif Jame Mosque,
Azimpur, Old Dhaka, 2018

welcoming manner. Visitors can rest and enjoy some conversation while passersby stop freely on the site. The upper courtyard leads to the "inner life" through the rhythmic placement of sculptural columns on the east and west wings. The panoramic view of the cemetery is contextualized by the realization of various thresholds: life and death, past and present, the individual and the community, heritage and contemporary living, memories and aspirations. After the traditional cleansing, male visitors enter the main prayer hall located parallel to the central courtyard along the west wing, while female visitors are welcomed on the upper level in the east wing along the courtyard. A transparent glass bridge defines the entire courtyard space and frames the view toward the cemetery located behind the mosque.

Upon entering the prayer hall, the *qibla* wall, in a serene brick texture, is highlighted by the skylight positioned along its entire length. The foreground is dominated by beautiful structural columns that simulate grand forest trees within the interior space. The subdued lighting serves to draw the visitors' attention to the wall and the direction of the Kaaba in Makkah. This remarkable play of light is realized by the intricate brick pattern in between the columns on the street façade that controls the rhythmic light. The columns also define a series of variations in the human drama of life, generated by the movements and personal aspects of the people in prayer at any given moment. Capitalizing on this first important public commission to showcase his talents for spatial composition and masterful applications of light and shadow, Azam filled the space with familiar and natural cues. Even within this densely urbanized setting, the exterior courtyard is bathed in variable sunlight and cleansed by an uplifting outlook of greenery and water bodies, where the breeze flows through to calm the spirit before the prayer ritual is performed. The "borrowed scenery" (*shakkei*) of this historic cemetery concludes the powerfully panoramic narrative of this special community space.

Shahid Haji Abdul Alim Playground (formerly known as "Balur Math" or sand field), located north of Lalbagh Fort in Old Dhaka, is another example of a gathering place alongside a public square, providing some respite amid this heavily congested neighborhood. The facility can be utilized throughout the year, especially when the rainy season hits Dhaka. Children, mothers, and the elderly can spend time reading and socializing under this roof, symbolizing a user-friendly opportunity for local unity. The material used here is the local brickwork and the landscaping is generous, with ivy-covered walls reminiscent of a bygone era. On the upper terrace, Azam positioned two large, indigenous trees that yield contrasting red and white blossoms, offering strategic shade and an inviting overview of the sporting activities down in the square. The main space in his community center is a recessed double-height void with a vaulted ceiling, creating a visual connection from the street to the square. This form is familiar to the local residents, where many of the public buildings from the colonial period still stand. The only contemporary intervention here is the steel pergola on the roof. Among the openings on the walls, Azam chose circular cutouts of various sizes to allow airflow throughout this shaded exterior section of the building, while the circular geometry on its brick walls becomes a symbol of harmony and a visual identity cue for locals of all ages.

Shahid Abdul Alim Playground, Old Dhaka, 2019

Shahid Abdul Alim Playground, Old Dhaka, 2019

On a site located at a busy intersection in Dhaka, Azam's three-story Azimpur Public Restrooms and library project (2020–2023) stands at one corner, out-scaled by a huge tree. The building is clad in a black, transparent exterior with double-height glazing that wraps around its second and third floors. This clearly contemporary interpretation distinguishes itself from other buildings in the vicinity, which have colonial or traditional design expressions on their façades. In fact, the whole structure is remarkably camouflaged, hardly catching the attention of passersby. Its design was carefully calculated to manifest the interior spaces on the upper floors while guaranteeing the privacy of its ground level. The ground floor is dedicated to a public restroom protected by a solid black wall clad in glazed ceramic tiles, indicating to passersby that this a discreet and hygienically maintained facility. It is easily accessible by a gentle ramp and the library and restaurant on the upper floor, overlooking a very busy junction, is an inviting solution to the otherwise ubiquitous problem of community amenities. The library is open to all and offers both private and public areas for reading and conversing alike, with opaque and transparent glazing. This visual and structural balance complements the project's various functions. The entire building is defined by a steel frame, partially free and without a solid volume, exposing the void allocated to a recreational terrace on the second level. This is a very high-profile site where pedestrian traffic, as well as vehicles of all kinds, posed a challenge to providing ease of entry and a certain degree of privacy and refuge for the community.

Azam's understanding of community needs and his experience in producing serene residential oases for the upper echelons of the urban population are brought to fruition in this very public and necessary project. In fact, he has generously provided a place to "escape" in the most unlikely and otherwise least favorable aspect of public construction. This brave and innovative solution will no doubt be challenged on a daily basis in the years to come.

Unfortunately, many public parks in Dhaka have become the perfect stage for the illegal drug scene and are a perennial problem for residents and local authorities alike. Osmani Udyan (2018–ongoing) is a prominent historical site in the heart of the city, near Osmani Udyan Lake and the Osmani Memorial Auditorium convention center. Once a gathering spot and playground for families, it has sadly metamorphosed into a danger zone. The Dhaka South City Corporation (DSCC) commissioned Azam to produce a master plan for its complete renovation, including new walkways connecting the neighborhoods on all sides, a library, a cafeteria, sports infrastructure, and food courts surrounding the lake. The feature structure he has designed is the museum and library complex, which is a brick-clad building with a series of decks, as well as a walkway for socializing but also for solitary contemplation. The water body, one of Azam's main architectural elements, strikes a masterful dialogue with the complex reaching the water below. This level difference between the park and the lake is skillfully mediated with the roof deck for visitors to enjoy. The result is a building quietly nestled alongside a series of island pods with planter boxes for trees and ivy floating in the foreground. On the adjacent shore, the backdrop acts as the *shakkei* ("borrowed scenery"), a technique used in Japanese landscape design to compose layers within the overall landscape context. Upon entering the complex, one strolls over a brick path that divides and reveals the three-dimensional nature of the design. Still on the roof level, visitors discover a fountain pool that relates the whole park to the lake hidden below.

Descending to the lower floor by the stairway, we finally recognize that the walkway is actually the roof level of this two-story building. Its main level has a long horizontal frontage to the lake with a *ghat* reaching out to the water. The interior spaces of the complex take in the view of the landscape, a conscious planning device to remind visitors of this unique setting. Ultimately, the synergy between the lake and the building in Osmani Udyan is a manifestation of Azam's many watercolor paintings, featuring vegetation and water bodies in the urban context of Dhaka.

communal harmony

AMIR
22

DELOWAR HOSSAIN AREA DEVELOPMENT

Lalbagh, Dhaka

2018–2024

This project is another revitalization initiative within the DSCC's "Jol Sobuje Dhaka" urban improvement charter. Located at the Kamrangirchar Shamshan Ghat in Kamrangirchar *Thana* (police district) in Old Dhaka and bordering the Buriganga River, this site is one of the largest slums in the city. It is known for its population density (circa 400,000 inhabitants), industrial activities, and serious environmental challenges. It is also near the historic Mughal garden established in 1670 AD. The original design brief was limited to a 4,082 m^2 playground area, and a budget was allocated accordingly by the Dhaka South City Corporation. After spending time with the local community, it was discovered that for a long time, this area was predominantly occupied by a Hindu community, with an open-to-sky crematorium, a Kali Goddess temple, and a Hindu graveyard with a polluted ritualistic pond next to it. With the passage of time, recent demographics show that Muslim inhabitants have increased significantly, whereas the Hindu community has been proportionally marginalized. Beside the field, there is also an existing mausoleum with a tomb of the local saint Hakim Jasim Uddin Maijvandari.

Conversations with residents revealed an undercurrent of conflict that was dealt with judiciously by ensuring both communities could gain a renewed sense of hope and prosperity. For a peaceful commencement, ancillary facilities were developed before attempting to revitalize the field. Due to the lack of additional funds, it was challenging to execute this architectural vision, but with determination the Ministry of Local Government and Rural Developments (LGRD) was finally engaged to explore funding possibilities. Eventually, the Ministry of Planning carefully reviewed the proposal and made physical investigations before passing it on to the final bureaucratic hurdle, the ECNEC (Executive Committee of the National Economic Council). The entire process was painstaking and took a year for its final approval.

pages 252–253
Swamp ground before renovation.

top
Barren ground before renovation.

bottom
Playing field after renovation.

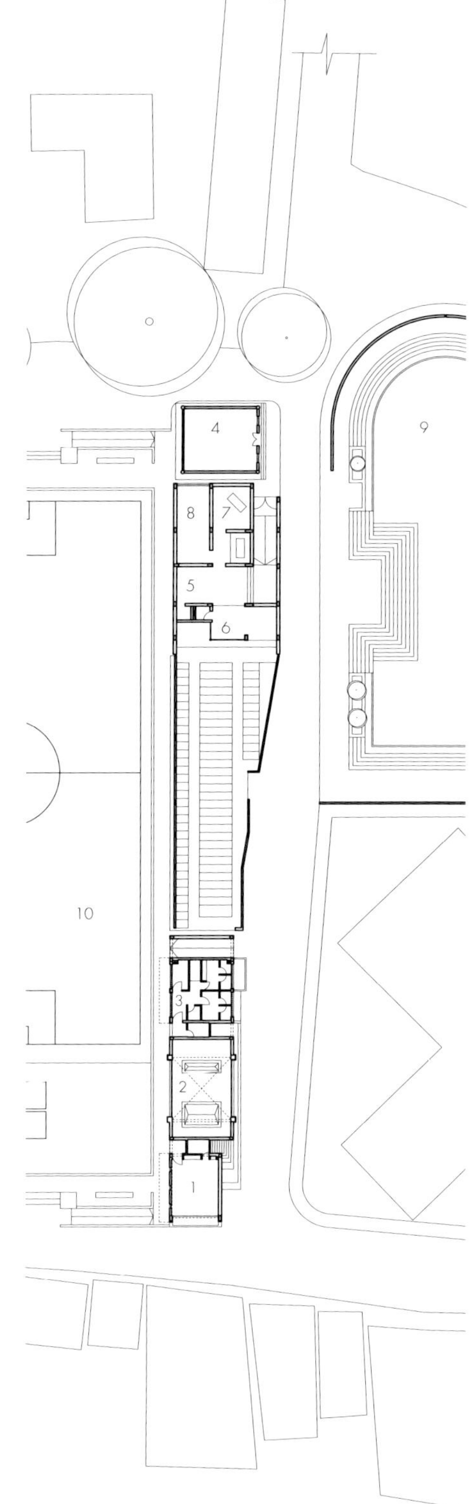

1. gym
2. mausoleum area
3. public restrooms
4. kali temple
5. electric crematorium room
6. ritual platform
7. manual burning area
8. generator room
9. pond
10. playground

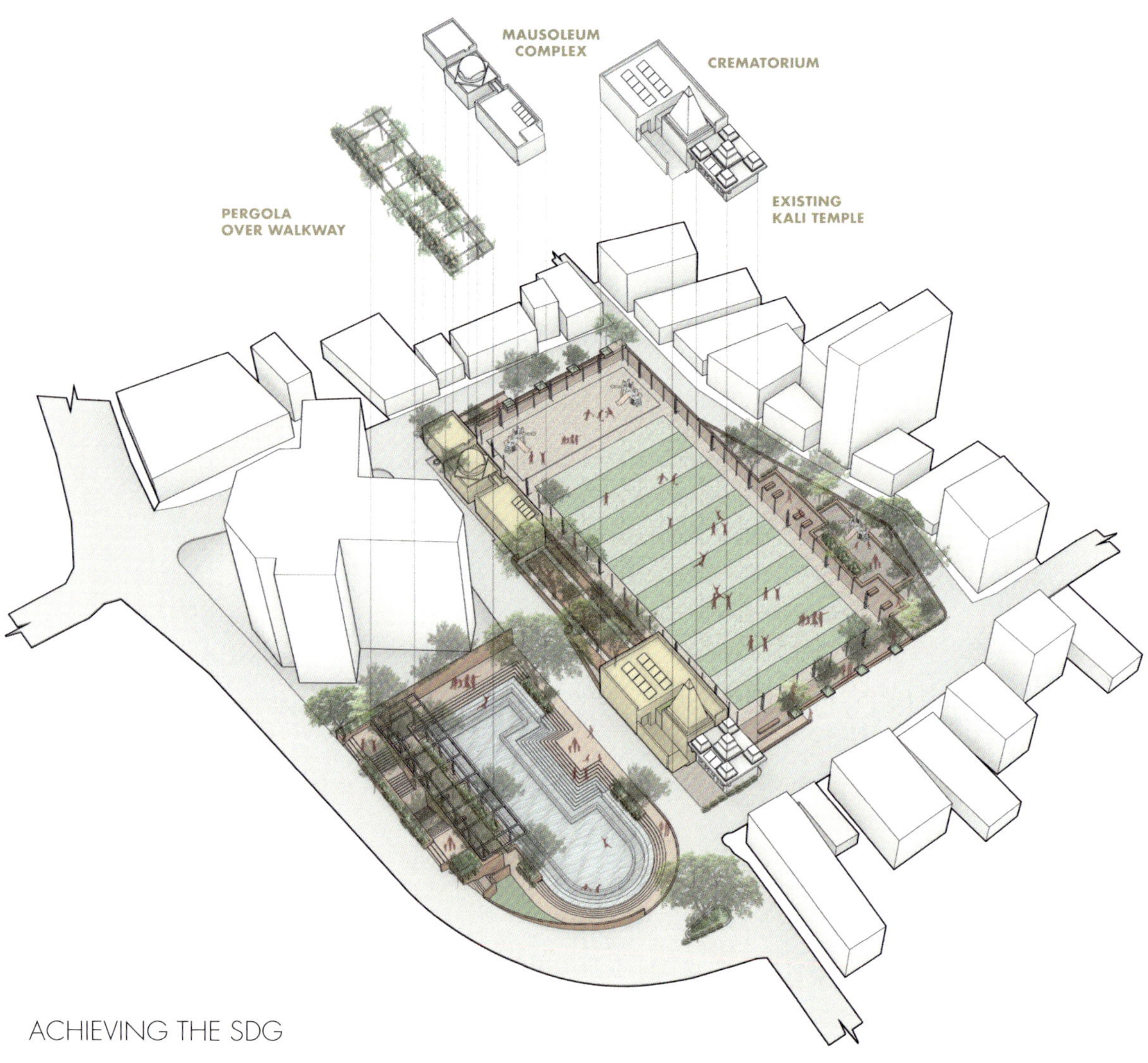

ACHIEVING THE SDG

Health and Well-Being

Delowar Hossain Area Development promotes health and well-being within the community. The newly planted trees enhance oxygen levels. The rainwater collected in the trench minimizes the accumulation of stagnant water, unlike before. The number of harmful insects and mosquitoes in the neighborhood has significantly decreased, which is reducing waterborne diseases.

Quality Education

Delowar Hossain Area Development has been thoughtfully designed and developed as a learning space for children, promoting both their physical and mental growth. They can explore and learn about various trees, and other flora and fauna. Additionally, experiencing all six seasons of Bangladesh in one place brings their lessons to life.
A library is proposed to be established where children, students, and professionals can spend their time reading and acquiring knowledge.

Gender Equality

In the evenings, this area becomes a vibrant community space where residents gather in a safe, well-lit environment. Women and adolescent girls now feel secure walking around and spending time there.

Clean Water and Sanitation

Previously, rainwater mixed with dirty water, causing waterborne diseases.
Now, rainwater is separated, collected in trenches, and filtered into free drinking water for the community. Meanwhile, the dirty water is directed separately, gradually draining out of the area through the city corporation's drainage system, improving overall sanitation.

Affordable and Clean Energy

Solar panels installed on the roof of this restored community building and temple create 1.2 kW of energy, which accounts for almost 50% of the building's requirement.

Decent Work and Economic Growth

The playground has created job opportunities, with three cleaners and one librarian appointed by the local authorities. This project has created economic growth for the local community.

Sustainable Cities and Communities

All the elements of this revitalization project provide improvements, including rainwater harvesting and treatment, safe water supplies to the neighboring mosque, a community building, free drinking water, social spaces for children and adults, a reading library space and a gymnasium. Together they create sustainable development for this community.

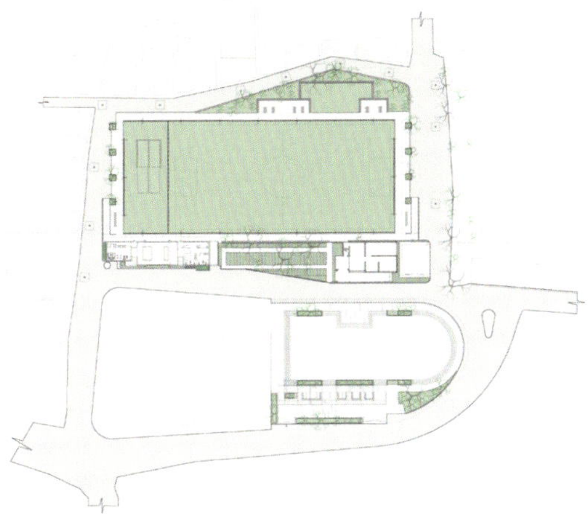

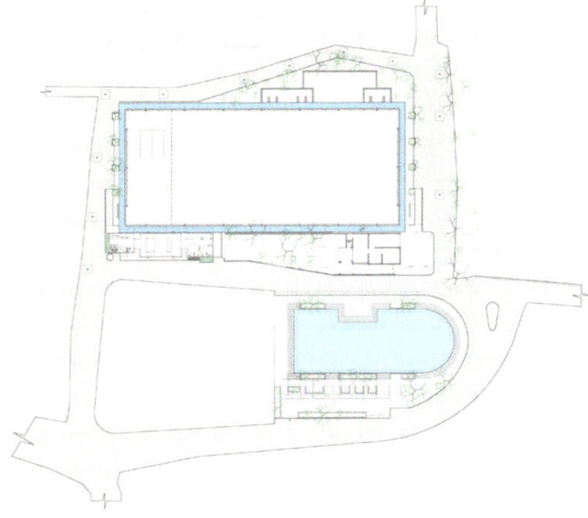

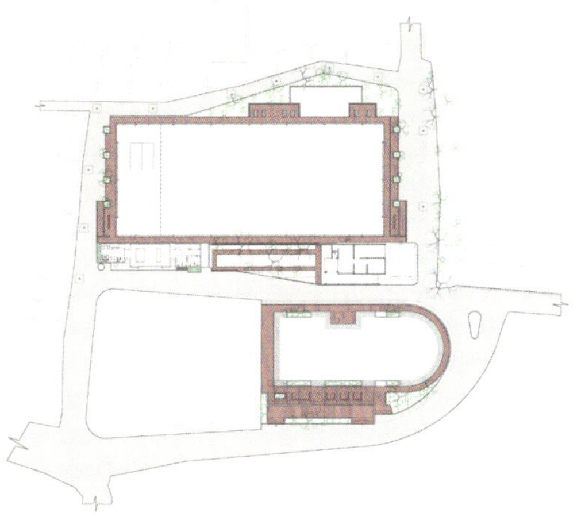

Climate Action

This park has developed opportunities for better environmental outcomes for the community by providing oxygen and reducing ccarbon dioxide. Adding more trees and better water management substantially reduces waterborne diseases.

Life Below Water

The pond within the complex serves as a vibrant ecosystem, supporting a sustainable fish-farming initiative led by the local community. This community-driven approach enhances food security, stimulates economic opportunity, and joins the conservation of local water-based ecosystems.

Life on Land

Children can now enjoy their rights to space and greenery, surrounded by birds and insects. They are free to play and socialize, which fosters better relationships with their families and neighbors and creates a sense of harmony.

Industry, Innovation, and Infrastructure

The water-collecting process and walkway for the people justify the innovation and infrastructure. The 6′x1.5′ slab for the trench was built at the site. The ground layer of the playing fields was covered with Astroturf since the park was being used heavily.

Partnerships for Goals

A strong partnership between the design team and the community was established from the very beginning of the project. Through numerous meetings, conversations, seminars, and other interactions, trust and respect were built between the community and the design team, enabling the project to be executed successfully.

Peace, Justice, and Strong Institutions

This place used to be filled with conflict, with people even carrying guns, but now that has completely disappeared. Today, the community's primary responsibility is to ensure peaceful living and justice for children, adolescents, women, and everyone else. We believe this has transformed into an unspoken but deeply ingrained institution.

Reduced Inequalities

Delowar Hossain Area Development provides a space for people of all backgrounds to connect, learn, and play together. The complex includes both a *mazar* and a temple, bringing two different religions into harmony. The playground fosters unity and community through its inclusive and welcoming environment.

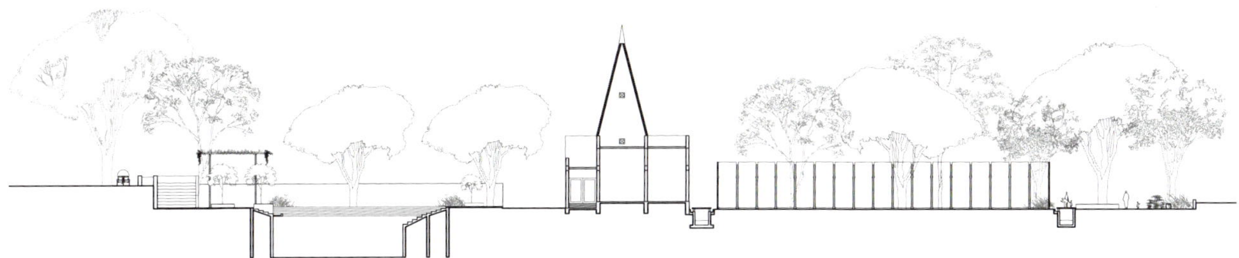

Pond Axis Sectional Elevation

Field Axis Sectional Elevation

previous page
Community pond after revitalization.

following pages

View of the new park in Old Dhaka.

It took four hundred years after the Mughals to create a patch of green on the edges of the Buriganga River.

scarcity to abundance

Before this revitalization project, this area suffered regular flooding, garbage accumulation, and unlicensed shops along its boundary wall, which caused a painful daily struggle for this community.

RASULBAGH SHISHU PARK

Azimpur, Dhaka

2018–2021

Rasulbagh Shishu Park is a revitalized public project located within the densely populated urban fabric of Old Dhaka. Part of the DSCC's "Jol Shobuje Dhaka" initiative, the project breathed new life into this previously derelict and poorly maintained public space. The park was accessible only by tight alleyways between narrow conglomerations of buildings. Residents suffered from very limited mobility, especially during the monsoon when the area was heavily flooded and unsanitary conditions were common due to the lack of effective drainage. Formerly walled off from the north side and used by vagrants and drug dealers, it deterred local families and children from visiting the park and the adjacent mosque on the southeast side. The wall was also used to support unlicensed stalls and shops, and an old, abandoned building stood in disrepair on the west side of the premises. The entire area was a source of anguish for the local community, both practically and socially.

Diligently developed and designed alongside the residents, the renovations began with the symbolic removal of the north wall. The park is now a proudly functioning representation of the kind of social cohesiveness its design aimed to foster. All the existing trees were preserved and many new ones and various other plants were established, mostly by the local children. This not only provides shade and protection from excess water but also acts as a kind of open-to-sky learning environment for children. Now boasting an open sports field, a children's playground and pavilion, a 500-meter "green" pathway, a public plaza for people to rest, a library, a gymnasium, a coffee shop, a community hall, an *Eidgah* (open prayer ground), and public restrooms, this park has become a truly welcoming and family-friendly space that fulfills multiple roles to the benefit of its community.

left
Conversation in the mosque within the park.

middle
Listening to the young people in the community.

right
Building a trench to harvest rainwater.

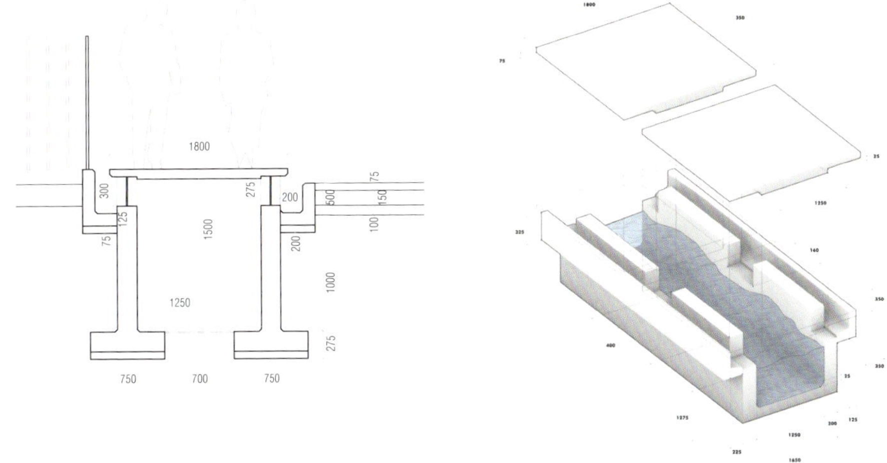

A 200-meter peripheral walkway was devised to include a water trench of 450,000-liter capacity, considering an average daily rainfall of 200 mm per hour during the monsoon season.
This innovative water harvesting and filtration system not only solved the problem of localized flooding, but also provided free drinking water for the residents—a true "gift from the park."

Views of the old park.

This project required very careful planning and intensive, cooperative efforts with the locals. The shared mindset revived what had previously been lost, instilling a sense of trust and respect among the residents of the area. The practical and culturally significant dismantling of the north wall not only provided around-the-clock accessibility and vigilance, but also restored faith and pride within the community.

Dismantling the wall of fear and disrespect.

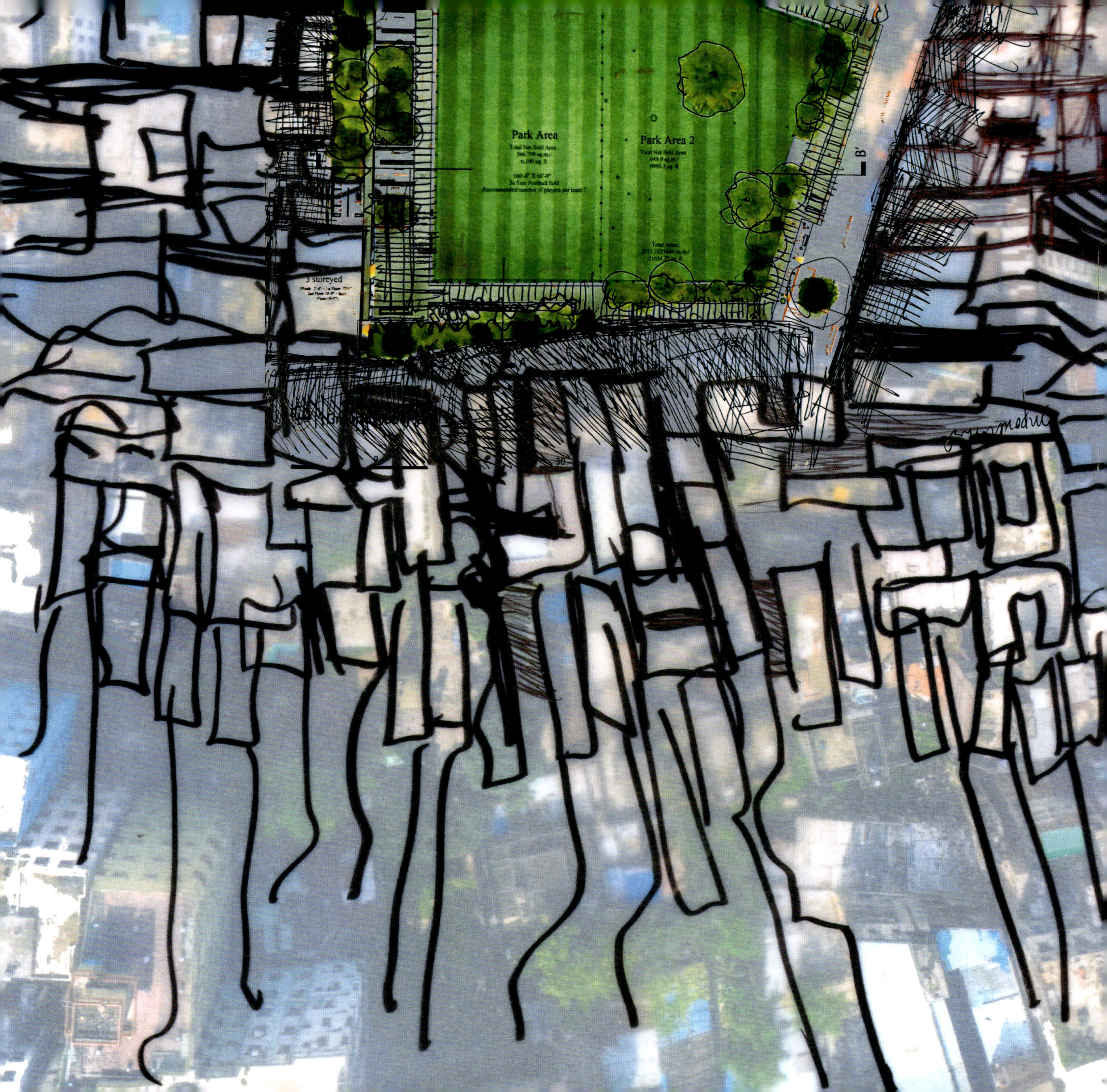
Park Area
Park Area 2
3 storeyed

from left to right
Collection of drinking water.
New community library.
Women's club and
children's activities.
Community celebrations.

previous page

top
A narrow secondary
entrance to the park.

bottom
Transformation after
dismantling the wall.

Section AA

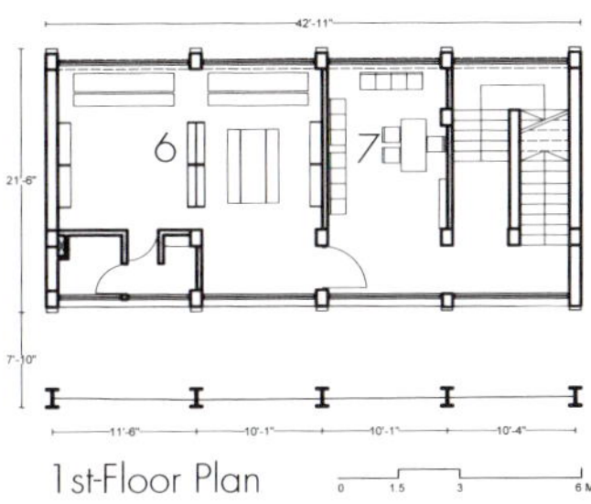

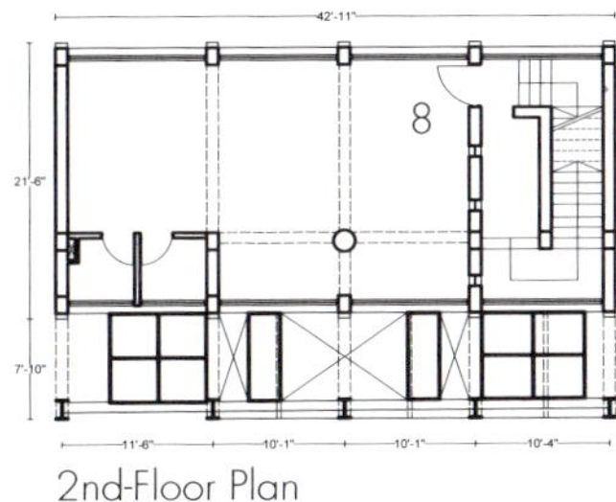

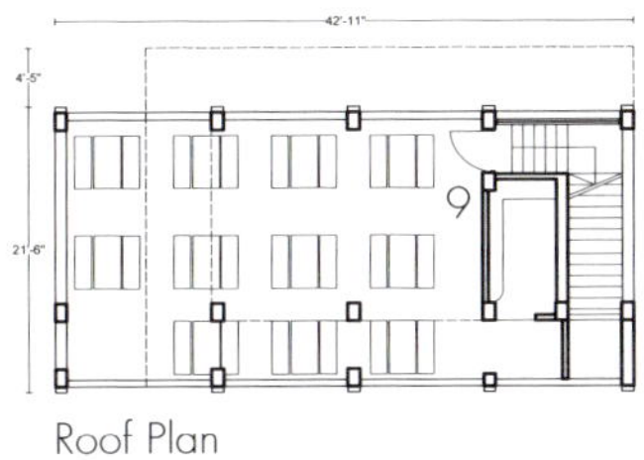

1. field area
2. new ablution space
3. mosque
4. motor control and water filter room
5. garbage disposal bins
6. library
7. councilor's room
8. gymnasium
9. children's weekend school

top
Park before renovation.

middle
Illegally occupied building before renovation.

bottom
Building and playing field after renovation.

Rain now becomes a natural celebration.

following pages
Annual Victory Day celebrations on December 16.

Children enjoying the space.

From scarcity to abundance.

urban pulse

HOTEL RANNA

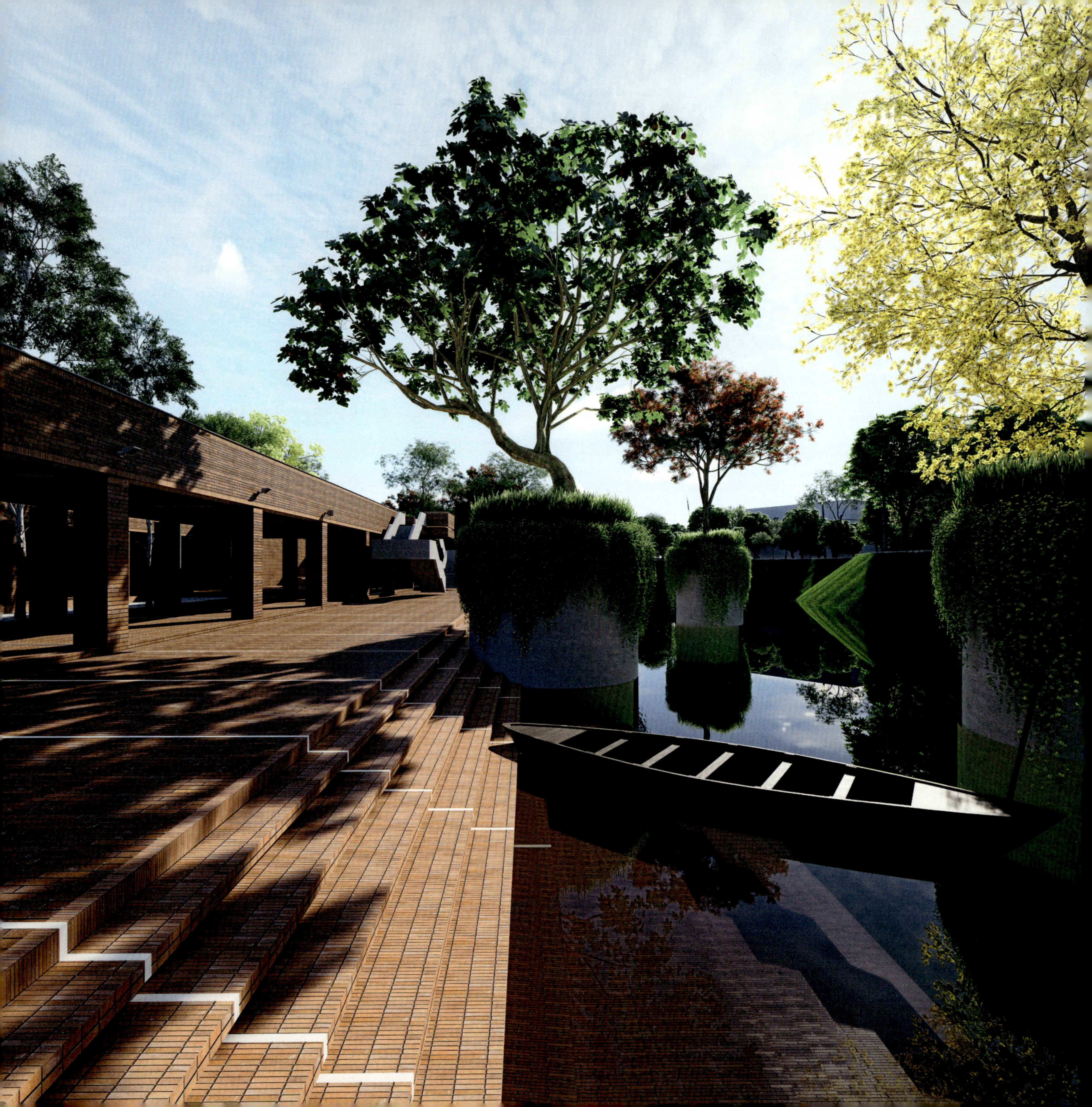

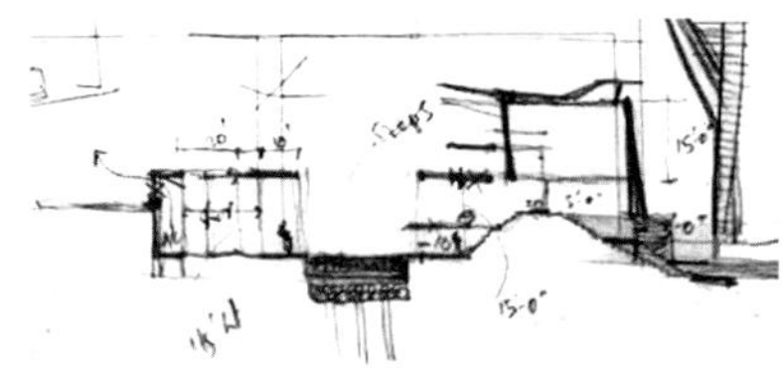

OSMANI UDYAN

Phoenix Road, Dhaka

2018–ongoing

Situated at the junction between the old and new city, bound by Phoenix Road, Abdul Gani Road, and Bangabandhu Avenue, the Secretariate, Police Headquarters, and the DSCC Headquarters, this site was a hub for illicit and antisocial activities. It seemed like a lost opportunity for the residents, as the large 23-acre parcel of land, though centrally located, did not benefit anyone. The area was previously visited for short-lived recreational purposes, so the design concept here is to encourage people to use the park as a vital bridge between the main city centers and the roads surrounding it, as a passageway and not simply a destination.

An in-depth investigation began on the site's potential and the preservation of its existing structures and large trees. Two water bodies were insufficient to collect the heavy rains and runoff to the park, so the first challenge was to locate the proposed promenade to minimize the felling of trees. The design was adapted and located on the existing water body. A new lake was carved out on two levels with recovered islands of trees. The upper level, 2 meters from the existing road, leads visitors to the other end of the park as a thoroughfare, and those who wish to spend more time there can access the lower level, which is 2.5 meters below the road level. This level houses car parking, food courts, a library, gymnasium, public restrooms, and *ghats* (steps) leading to the pond. A new bus stop has been designed at the eastern edge to facilitate connectivity and to further entice people to spend time in this rejuvenated green space in the heart of the city, especially at night, with ample lighting ensuring a safe haven for all. To prevent the carrying of bottled water and the use of plastic in public places, this design ensures a rainwater harvesting system that collects 2.5 million gallons into a trench under the walkways. The water is then filtered and provided as drinking water for visitors through the provision of water fountains and dispensers at strategic intervals.

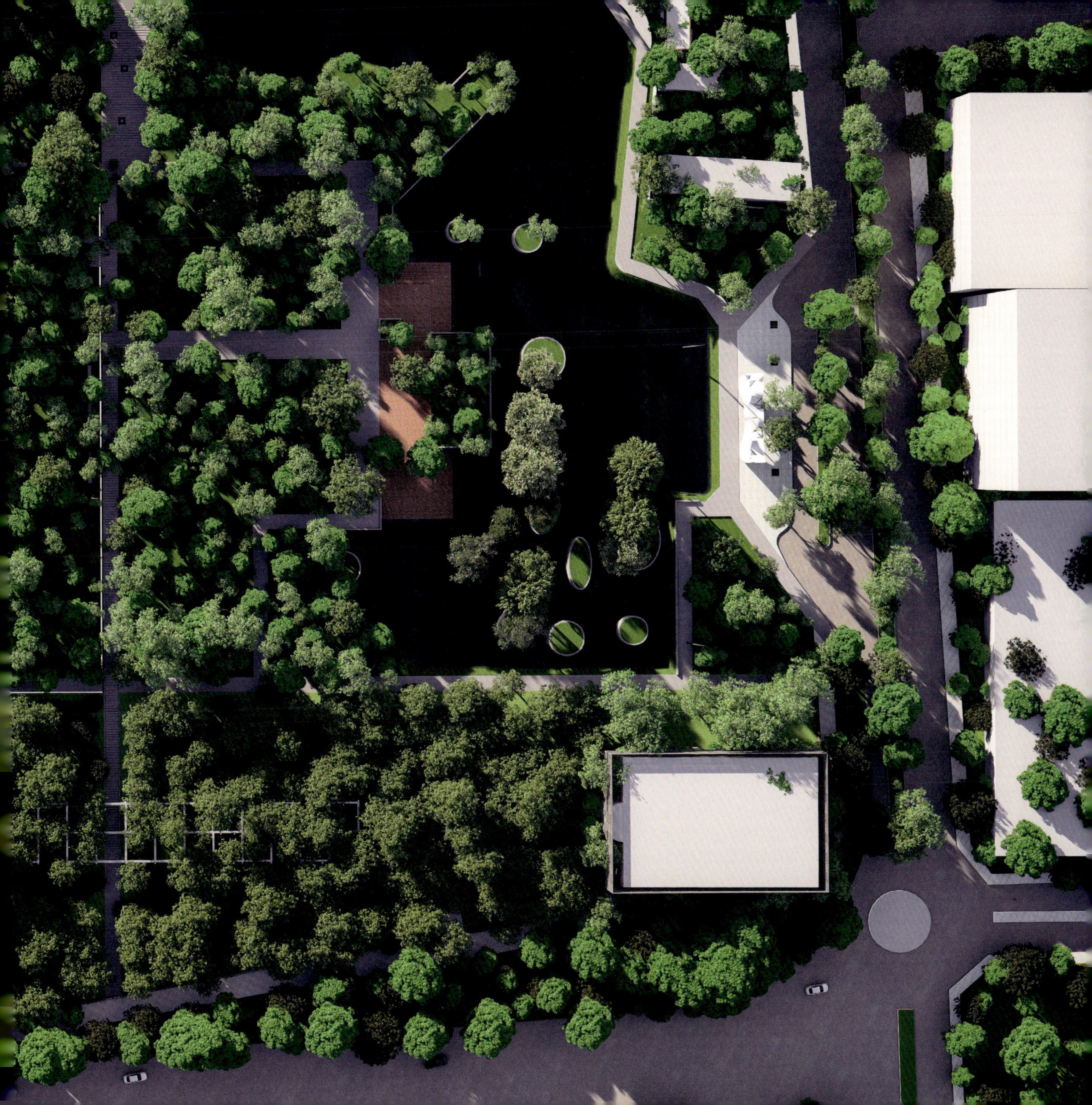

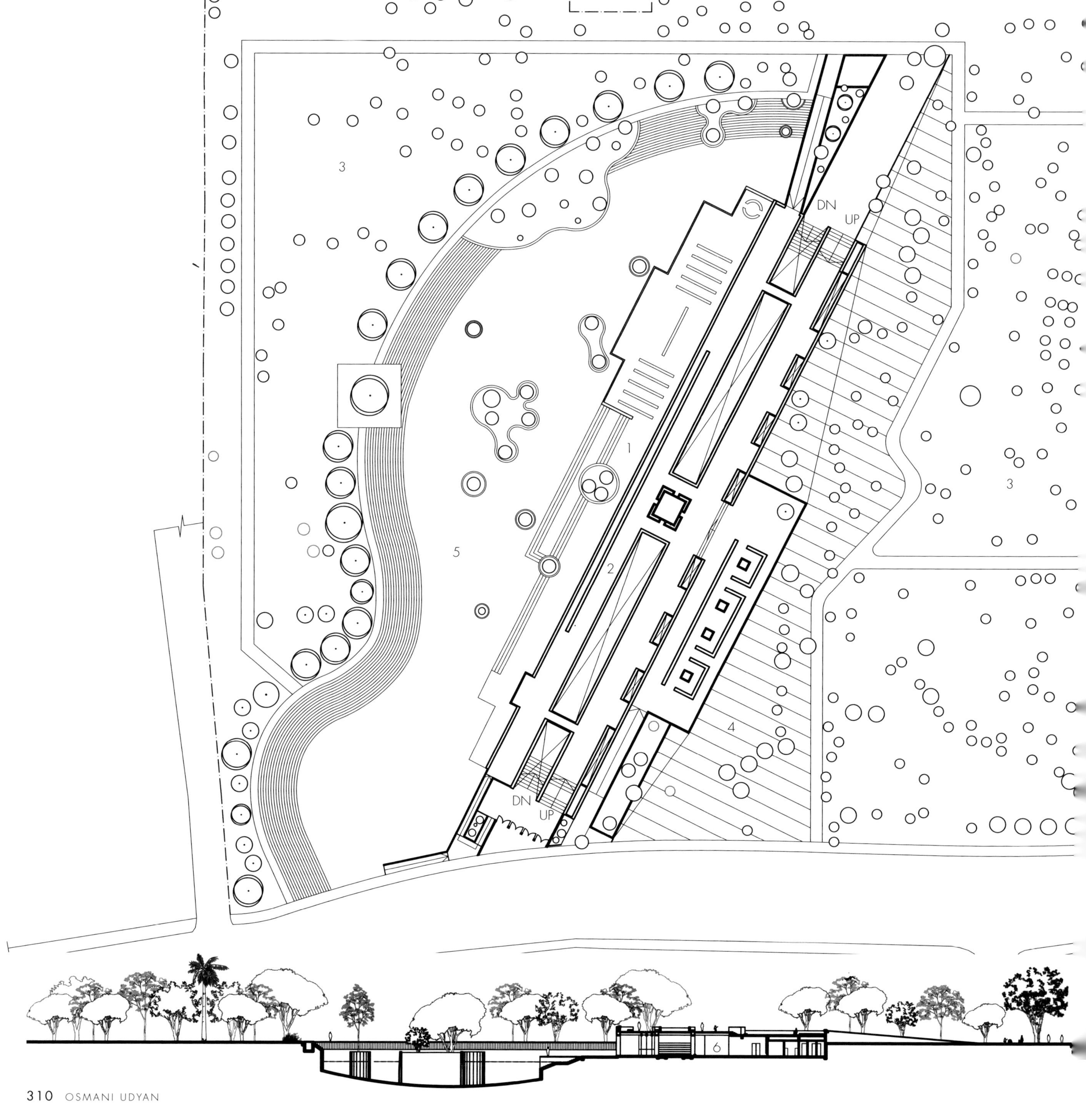
3
DN
UP
1
3
5
2
4
DN
UP
6

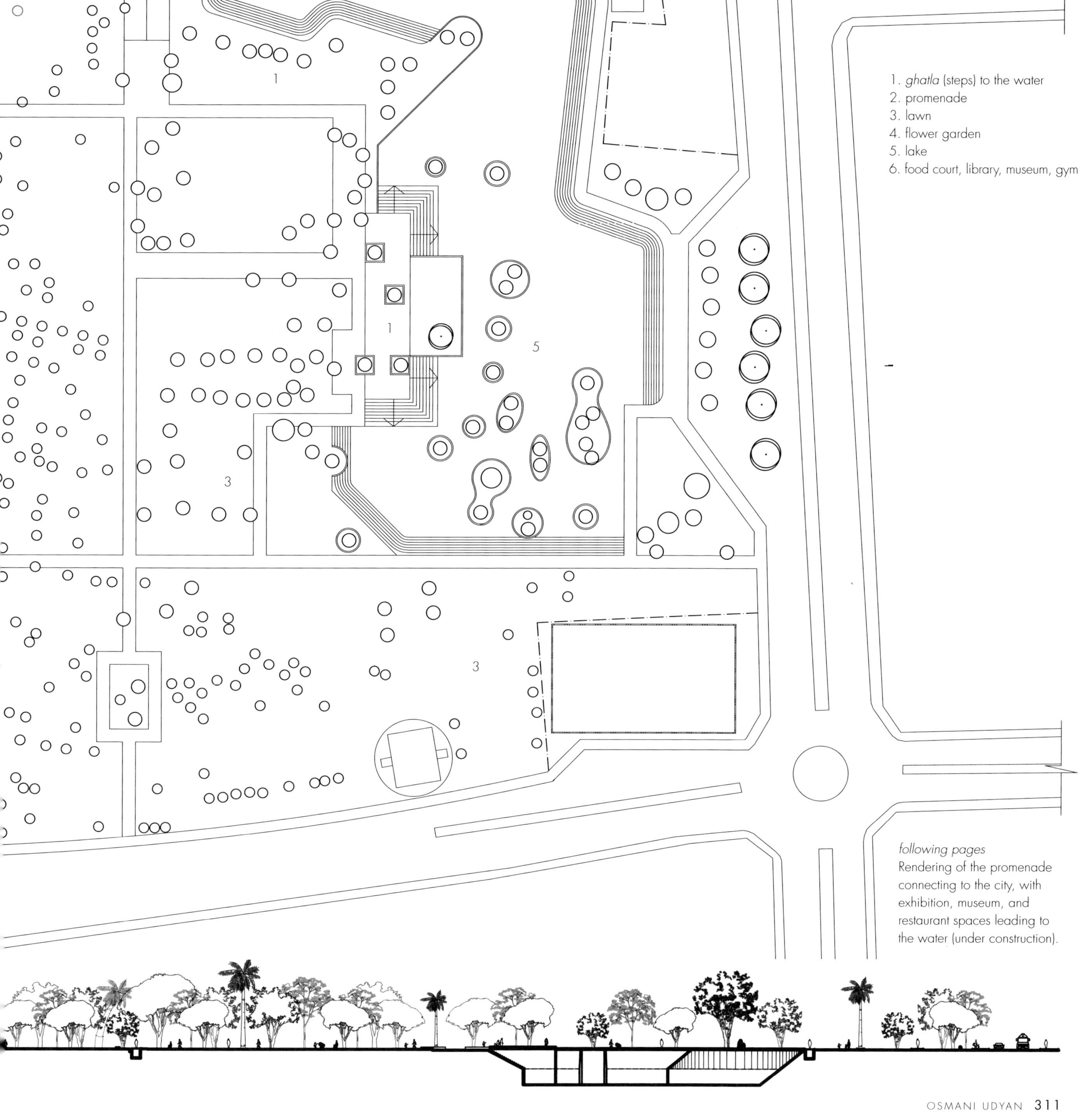

1. *ghatla* (steps) to the water
2. promenade
3. lawn
4. flower garden
5. lake
6. food court, library, museum, gym

following pages
Rendering of the promenade connecting to the city, with exhibition, museum, and restaurant spaces leading to the water (under construction).

Image courtesy of *The Fame* magazine, 2024

BIOGRAPHY

Md. Rafiq Azam is an internationally acclaimed architect living and working in Bangladesh. In 1995, he founded his own practice, Shatotto—architecture for green living, based in Dhaka, and has since developed a remarkable signature style based on the fusion of local traditions and mysticism with the country's unique ecosystems and natural endowments. Azam's particular design mastery with light and shadow, water and air, is influenced by his watercolor painting practice as well as the Bengali literature of Lalon Shah, iconic poet and social reformer, and Rabindranath Tagore, Renaissance polymath and painter.

Azam's green architecture is uniquely conceived as a process of "energy gaining." His recent interventions in urban architecture, especially parks and playgrounds, have transformed entire sections of Old Dhaka. This localized revitalization movement has initiated a complex dialogue among politicians, economists, social leaders, and construction industries to ensure healthier communities.

AWARDS IN ARCHITECTURE

2025

Winner – Urban Land Institute, Asia Pacific Awards for Excellences

Winner – Public Spaces Category – Monsoon Architecture Awards

2023

Gold Award – International Design Awards

Silver Award – International Design Awards
Honourable Mention – International Design Awards

2022

Robert Matthew Lifetime Achievement Award – Commonwealth Association of Architects (CAA)

Winner – Urban Landscape Category – World Architecture Festival Awards

Winner – Social Development Category – LFB Leadership Excellence Award

High Commendation – AR Public Award

Winner – 12th Idea Tops Award, China

High Commendation – UIA 2030 Award

2021

Platinum Category – Outstanding Property Award, London

Honourable Mention – DNA Paris Design Awards

2020

Gold Diploma in Architecture – Eurasian Prize

Silver Diploma in Urban Planning – Eurasian Prize

2019

Winner – Top 10 Green Buildings of the Decade – Malaysia GBC Awards

2017

Gold Medal – ARCASIA

Winner – World Architecture Festival Awards

Winner – Cityscape Global Award

Winner – Berger Award for Excellence in Architecture

Co-Winner – Berger Award for Excellence in Architecture

2016

Rise High Bangladesh – Amazing Bangladeshi Award

Most Influential Names in Architecture in the Subcontinent – AD50

Commendation – PAM Green Excellence Awards, Malaysia

Nomination – Aga Khan Award for Architecture

2015

Honourable Mention – ARCASIA Award

Nomination – Aga Khan Award for Architecture

2014

Classic Excellence Award – Malaysia

2013

Green Planet Architect for Sustainable Architecture Award, Dominican Republic

2012

Winner – South Asian Architect of the Year Award

Winner – Emirates Glass Leading European Architects' Forum (LEAF) Award

Winner – 11th Cycle – World Architectural Community Award

2011

Commendation – South Asian Architecture Award

Commendation – Berger Award for Excellence in Architecture

2009

Winner – Cityscape Architectural Review Award

High Commendation – Cityscape Architectural Review Award

Shortlisted – Leading European Architects Forum (LEAF) Awards

Shortlisted – Health & Residential Category, World Architecture Festival Awards

Long Listed – Residential Category – World Architecture News (WAN) Awards

Winner – 5th Cycle – World Architectural Community Award

Citation – 3rd Cycle – World Architectural Community Award

2008

Winner – 2nd Cycle – World Architectural Community Award

Winner – 1st Cycle – World Architectural Community Award

Selected – Ten Emerging Designers of the World – Urban Land, USA

Recognition – Emerging Heroes of Bangladesh – *New Age* Newspaper, Bangladesh

2007

Winner – Berger Award for Excellence in Architecture

Commendation – AR Emerging Architecture Awards

Honourable mention – Kenneth F. Brown, Asia Pacific Culture & Architecture Design Award, USA

Finalist – Aga Khan Award for Architecture

Recognition – 27 Power Players of Bangladesh – *ICE Today* magazine, Bangladesh

2005

Commendation – South Asian Architecture Award

2004

Commendation – Cityscape Architectural Review Award

Finalist – Aga Khan Award for Architecture

Nomination – Aga Khan Award for Architecture

2003

Commendation – South Asian Architecture Award

1999

Winner – Young Architect Category – South Asian Architecture Award

1997

Commendation – South Asian Architecture Award

1996

Winner – Design – Institute of Architects Bangladesh (IAB)

1992

Nomination – Aga Khan Award for Architecture

1991

Winner – Mimar International Design Competition VII, London

AWARDS IN PAINTING

1989

Winner – Young Artists Painting Competition, Association Development Agencies of Bangladesh (ADAB)

1981

Diploma Certificate—International Competition for Young Artists, USSR

1978

Shaheed Smriti Award – Contribution in the Field of Art in Bangladesh

Silver Medal – Shankar's International Children's Competition, India

1977

First Prize – National Children's Television Award (*Notun Kuri*), Bangladesh

Bronze Medal – Shankar's International Children's Competition, India

1976

Jawaharlal Nehru Memorial Gold Medal – Shankar's International Children's Competition, India

INVITED KEYNOTE SPEAKER

2025

"Ignited Minds," Apeejay Festival of Ideas, organized by Apeejay School of Architecture, Greater Noida, Uttar Pradesh, India

Dealer Conference, Cairo, Egypt

IAPEX—Lahore Chapter, Lahore, Pakistan

"Green Architecture as Social Change Maker," LafargeHolcim Bangladesh PLC

"Architecture: Where to Go?," BSRM, Dhaka, Bangladesh

2024

CAA conference, Rwanda

"Mosque Architecture: Globality of Place," organized by Abdullatif Alfozan Award for Mosque Architecture

"Architectural Praxis at Confluence of Disciplinary Boundaries," North South University, Dhaka

2023

India Art, Architecture & Design Biennale, Ministry of Culture, Delhi, India

"Design Perspectives," FOAID, Indore, India

"Design Perspectives," FOAID, Kolkata, India

"Fire-Safe Glazing for Architecture," organized by Grasshopper Group, Dhaka

2022

Jaipur Architecture Festival, organized by CDOS, RIICO & FICCI, Rajasthan, India

Rajasthan Architecture Festival, organized by Indian Institute of Architects, Delhi

2021

Military Institute of Science & Technology

"Impact of Infrastructure on Students in Modern-Day Institutional Learning," organized by IQAC, USTC

WAC India

Context BD

Teachers Training Program in collaboration with Council of Architecture-Training & Research Centre (COA-TRC), Kolhapur, India

2020

Taylor's University Architecture Graduate Showcase

2017

MIPIM, Cannes, Green Planet Architects, France

MAHA Conference, IIA Maharashtra Chapter, India

2016

Annual Festival Melange, Indubhai Parekh School of Architecture

Silver Jubilee of IIID Nashik Regional Chapter, India

"Architecture and Anxieties of Location," New York, USA

"Architecture in Landscape," Bengal Institute, Dhaka

MERAKI – Design Dynamics, Baliram Hirary College of Architecture, India

Arch Fest, Dept. Architecture, State University of Bangladesh

"Architecture for Green Living," Dept. Architecture, North South University, Dhaka

ARCH 102 Talk Series, NASA, India

2015

"Rethinking Architecture Education and Practice," Ahsanullah University of Science and Technology, Dhaka

2013

Forum for Exchange & Excellence in Design, Pune, India

Center for Environmental Planning & Technology, Ahmedabad, India

2012

Forum CSA (Alumni of the City School of Architecture), Sri Lanka, Dept. Architecture, Moratuwa University, Sri Lanka

Master Architect Lecture Series: C.A.R.E. School of Architecture, Trichy, India

Shibpur Engineering University, Kolkata, India

Daud College, Karachi, Pakistan

National Institute of Advanced Studies in Architecture, Cuttack, India

361 Degree Conference, Mumbai, India

3rd International Seminar & Exhibition, Builders Academy Australia, Melbourne, Australia

Mongolbar Shobha, Dhaka, Bangladesh

Jadavpur University, Kolkata, India

2011

T2F, The Atelier, Karachi, Pakistan

Architect's Forum, Aga Khan Trust, London, UK

Bangladesh University, Dhaka, Bangladesh

Masa Conference, Bangalore, India

Mongolbar Shobha, Dhaka, Bangladesh

2010

Commonwealth Association of Architects Conference, Colombo, Sri Lanka

Institute of Architects Bangladesh, Dhaka

Asian Congress of Architects, Lahore, Pakistan

"Comsets," NCA and IAP Islamabad, Pakistan,

Pertubuhan Akitek Malaysia (PAM), Kuala Lumpur, Malaysia

Indian Institute of Architects, Kerala, India

Jadavpur University, Kolkata, India

Universiti Teknology Malaysia, Kuala Lumpur, Malaysia

2009

Metro City Summit, Kuala Lumpur, Malaysia

2008

"My Tropical Architecture," Kuala Lumpur Vision, Malaysia

Australian Institute of Architects, Sydney, Australia

Architecture Conference, Reggio Calabria University, Italy

Architecture Conference, National University of Singapore, Singapore

Architecture Conference, Jadavpur University, Kolkata, India

2007

Young Architect's Festival, Kolkata, India

IAP Annual Conference, Karachi, Pakistan

National College of Arts, Lahore, Pakistan

Jahangirnagar University, Dhaka, Bangladesh

Institute of Architects Bangladesh, Dhaka

2006

University of Hawaii, Manoa, USA

Catholic University of America, Washington D.C., USA

"Datum: KL Conference," Kuala Lumpur, Malaysia

University of Malaysia, Kuala Lumpur, Malaysia

2004

Conference, South Asian Association for Regional Cooperation of Architects, Dhaka, Bangladesh

VISITING FACULTY MEMBER

2025–2006

BRAC University, Bangladesh

2020

Curtin University, Australia

2011

Department of Architecture, NED, Karachi, Pakistan

2006–2011

Jadavpur University, Kolkata, India

2009

National University Singapore, Department of Architecture, Singapore

2007

North South University, Department of Architecture, Dhaka

2006–2000

University of Asia Pacific, Department of Architecture, Dhaka

1998 –1996

Ahsanullah University of Science & Technology, Department of Architecture, Dhaka

JUROR

2024

World Architecture Festival, Singapore

CAA Awards Programme, Rwanda

2023

Monsoon Architecture Awards, IIA Cochin Centre, Cochin, India

World Architecture Festival (WAF) Awards, Singapore

2021

AESA, Pune, India

Heritage Pictogram: Visual Storytelling Competition, organized by Context BD

IAB Design Award

2020

"Faith," Urban Design Architectural Competition, UNI

2016

"Mohammedi Park Housing Society," Karachi, Pakistan

2013

School of Architecture, Pune, India

Masjid MACMA Architecture

Master Jury, ARCASIA Award for Architecture

2011

Competition, Malaysian Institute of Architects, Malaysia

Agrani Bank Head Office Design Competition, Dhaka, Bangladesh

Master jury, ARCASIA Award for Architecture

WORKSHOPS & EXHIBITIONS

2019

"Bengal Stream, Over the World," Bengal Institute of Architecture, Dhaka

2017

MIPIM, Palais des festival, Cannes, France

2016

Dhaka Art Summit, Bangladesh

2014

"Time Space Existence," Collateral Event at Palazzo Bembo, Biennale Architettura, Venice

2013

Bangladesh University, Dhaka

2012

Next Residence, Kerala, India

Jadavpur University, India

Chittagong University of Engineering and Technology, Bangladesh

2009

"Two Men Show," Gallery Hittite, Yorkville Art District, Toronto, Canada

2008

"Nature Is" Exhibition, Bengal Gallery, Dhaka

"Architectural Excellence in Bangladesh," AIA Exhibition, Sydney, Australia

2007

"AR Emerging Architecture" Exhibition, RIBA, London, UK

Kenneth Brown Worldwide Travel Exhibitions

2005

UIA, Architectural Exhibition, Istanbul, Turkey

1999

"arTchitecture" solo exhibition, Drik Gallery, Dhaka

1998

"arTchitecture" solo exhibition, New York, USA

1995

Solo Painting Exhibition, Kathmandu, Nepal

8th ARCASIA Forum Architectural Exhibition, Singapore

1994

10th National Young Artists Exhibition, Dhaka

1993

6th Asian Art Biennial, Bangladesh

1986

3rd Asian Art Biennial, Bangladesh

1985

7th National Painting Exhibition, Bangladesh

SELECTED BIBLIOGRAPHY

2025

Somokal, Eid Shongkha, March 2025

DOT: Art & Architecture Journal, Bangladesh, April 2025: SHL Regal, pp. 13–18.

2024

La Croix, newspaper, France: Architect Rafiq Azam

The Daily Star, Your Property Guru, quarterly ed., Bangladesh, January 2024: In Conversation with Architect Rafiq Azam, pp. 54, 56–57.

2023

Prestige Magazine, Bangladesh, June 2023: Celebrating Architectural Excellence: Architects' Symposium, pp. 2–3.

Universal Acquaintance, Towards a Contemporary View of Mosque Architecture, first ed., Saudi Arabia, 2023: Mayor Mohammad Hanif Jame Mosque, pp. 230–243.

2022

The Architectural Review, UK, July/August 2022: Rasulbagh Shishu Park, pp. 80–87.

Ceramic Bangladesh, Bangalore, June 2022: Transforming Times, pp. 30–38.

2021

TIME Magazine, October 28, 2021: "Climate Resilience Is a Design Challenge: This Bangladeshi Architect Has Solutions"

DOT: Art & Architecture Journal, Bangladesh, January–March 2021: Mayor Mohammad Hanif Jame Mosque, pp. 21–29.

2020

Harper's Bazaar Arabia, December 14, 2020: "How This Architect Is Combining Sustainable Design and Luxury"

Modern Architecture, A Critical History, fifth ed., London, 2020: Bangladesh Chancery Complex in Islamabad, Pakistan, pp. 482–485.

Showcase, An Architectural Magazine, Bangladesh, December 2020: Mayor Mohammad Hanif Jame Mosque, pp. 26–32.

Religious Facilities, Spain, 2020: Mayor Mohammad Hanif Jame Mosque, pp. 300–311.

2019

Showcase, Architectural Magazine, Bangladesh, July 2019: South Basera, pp. 28–35.

"SA Family Graveyard," *The New York Times, Style and Travel Magazine*, USA, May 2019, p. 64.

2018

"Design Detail," *The Architecture Magazine*, Kerala, India, August 2018: Nikunja Residence, pp. 14–17.

"Design Detail," *The Architecture Magazine*, Kerala, India, August 2018: Huda's Skyline, pp. 18–21.

"Design Detail," *The Architecture Magazine*, Kerala, India, August 2018: SA Family Graveyard, pp. 22–24.

2017

DOT: Art & Architecture Journal, Bangladesh, December 2017: Huda's Skyline, pp. 13–17.

DOT: Art & Architecture Journal, Bangladesh, June 2017: SA Family Graveyard, pp. 21–27.

DOT: Art & Architecture Journal, Bangladesh, June 2017: Nikunja Residence, pp. 29–34.

2016

Architectural Digest, Conde Nast India, March–April 2016: Shatotto, p. 190.

2015

Design Detail 12, vol. 2, Bangalore, April 2015: Assemblage of Gen-Next Architects, pp. 48–49.

Design Detail 12, vol. 2, Bangalore, April 2015: Brushstrokes of Imagination on the Canvas of a City, pp. 86–90.

2014

ICE Today, Bangladesh, April 2014: An Architect by Chance: In Conversation with Rafiq Azam, pp. 39–41.

Jamini, An international art magazine, Winter 2014: An Architect by Chance: In Conversation with Rafiq Azam, pp. 180–184.

Casa Vogue, Milan, April 2014: Interview by Stefania Ragusa, p. 46.

2013

Rafiq Azam Architecture for Green Living, Rosa Maria Falvo (ed.), Skira Editore, 2013, Milan, Italy

Bondhon 36, vol. 4, Bangladesh, April 2013: Mizan Residence, SA Residence, South Water Garden, Karim Residence, Meghna Residence, pp. 4–15.

Archipendium, Germany, 2013: SA Residence, pp. 7–8.

Documentary by Mara Corradi and Roberto Ronchi, sponsored by floornature.com: *Rafiq Azam: Architecture for Green Living*

Daybeds, vol. 133, Bangkok, 2013: Architect for Green Living, *Daybeds* magazine, vol. 133, Bangkok, 2013, pp. 226–231.

2012

Indian Architects and Builders, IA&B 8, vol. 25, India, April 2012: Profile of Rafiq Azam, pp. 88–98.

The Journal of the Indian Institute of Architects 4, vol. 77, India, April 2012: SA Residence, pp. 63–68.

Indian Architects and Builders, IA&B 10, vol. 25, India, June 2012: Profile of Rafiq Azam, Azam Residence, Meghna Residence, Mizan Residence, SA Residence, pp. 50–81.

Inside Outside 327, India, September 2012: SA Residence, Interview, pp. 122–31.

Next Residence, Indian Institute of Architects, Thrissur Center, India, September 2012: Profile of Rafiq Azam, SA Residence

The Hindu, India, September 28, 2012: Architecture Models for Kerala showcase.

Daily Star Lifestyle 50, vol. 7, Bangladesh, December 25, 2012: Profile of Rafiq Azam, SA Residence, Khazedewan Apartments, Meghna Residence

Designer + Builder 91, vol. 10, India, December 2012: SA Residence, Mizan Residence, Meghna Residence, Azam Residence, South Water Caress, Family Graveyard, pp. 84–100.

New Concept Urban Landscape, China, December 2012: SA Residence, pp. 274–79.

Architecture + Interior, Pakistan, 2012: SA Residence, pp. 40–45.

C3 339, South Korea, 2012: SA Residence, pp. 68–75.

Beton 2, Czech Republic, 2012: SA Residence, pp. 40–45.

Sthappattyo Amra 1, vol. 1, Bangladesh, 2012: Interview, Azam Residence, Haroon Residence, pp. 7–11.

2011

Shilparup 4/4, Bangladesh, October–December 2010: South Water Garden, South Wonder Apartments, South Water Caress, Alif Breeze Apartments, pp. 74–83.

Architecture Asia, Journal of the Architects Regional Council, Arcasia 2, Malaysia, April, May, June 2011: Interview, South Water Caress, pp. 16–21.

The Journal of the Indian Institute of Architects 6, vol. 76, India, June 2011: Alif Breeze Apartments, pp. 54–56.

Bangla Today, Bangladesh, July 2011: Cover story, Interview, SA Residence, pp. 10–12.

Bari Ghor, supplement of *Shokaler Khobor, Bangladesh*, August 2011: Profile of Rafiq Azam, SA Residence, pp. 1–6.

Archi Times 10, vol. 27, Pakistan, October 2011: Poetry and Mysticism in Architecture, p. 6.

Indian Architect and Builder, IA&B 3, Architect's Mention, 361 Degree Conference, vol. 25, India, November 2011: p. 43

Archi Times 11, vol. 27, Pakistan, November 2011: Interview, SA Residence, South Water Caress, Bangladesh Chancery, Mizan Residence, pp.13–17.

The Daily Star, Bangladesh, December 2011: Photo Exhibition on Excellence in Architecture

Archives 1, Bangladesh, December 2011: Alif Breeze Apartments, pp. 39–46.

2009

Kali o Kalam 12, vol. 5, Bangladesh, January 2009: Mahmud Residence, Gulfeshan, Mizan Residence, pp. 86–90.

Shilparup, 2, vol. 3 (Bangladesh, April–June 2009): Special issue dedicated to Rafiq Azam: Drik Gallery: Interview, Meghna Residence, South Wonder Apartments, Karim Residence, Khazedewan Apartments, Alif Breeze Apartments, South Water Garden, Islami Eye Hospital, SPL Nilambori Apartments, Coral Reef Heritage, Azam Residence, SPL Chandrima, pp. 2, 6, 7, 14–36.

Architecture Plus, UAE, 2009: Profile of Rafiq Azam, Meghna Residence, pp. 50–53.

Atelier Crisis Creative Think Tank, Spain, 2009: Mizan Residence, pp. 14–15.

The Plan 54, Italy, 2009: SA Residence, pp. 78–90.

2008

Ada, Architecture Design Art, Pakistan, vol.1, January–February 2008: Meghna Residence, pp. 74–85.

Architecture Asia, ARCASIA Journal, Malaysia, Issue 2, April–June 2008: South Wonder, pp. 52–55.

Architecture Asia, ARCASIA Journal, Malaysia, Issue 3, July–September 2008: South Water Garden, pp. 54–55.

Urban Land, USA, vol. 67, No. 11/12, November–December 2008: Profile on Rafiq Azam, Khazedewan Apartment, p. 62.

2007

Architecture Asia, Journal of Architects Regional Council Asia (ARCASIA), Issue 3, July 2007–September 2007, Malaysia: Meghna Residence, pp. 8–11.

AD—Made In India, UK, Profile No. 190, vol. 77, No. 6 November/December 2007: Gulfeshan Apartments, Meghna Residence, Mizan Residence, p. 123.

The Architectural Review, UK, December 2007: Mizan Residence, p.12.

Shilparup, Bangladesh, 2007: South Water Garden, Alif Breeze, pp. 75–83.

Financial Times, England, London: AR Emerging Architectural Award, 2007

2006

Stappathya O Nirman, No. 12, Bangladesh, January–March 2006: Haroon Residence, Khazedewan Apartment, pp. 39–49.

Indian Architects and Builders, IA&B, India, vol. 19 (06), February 2006: Mizan Residence, Karim Residence, pp. 76–81.

Architecture Asia, ARCASIA Journal, Malaysia, June–September 2006: Khazedewan Apartment

New Straits Times, Malaysia, July 2006: Gulfeshan, Khazedewan Apartment, Mizan Residence, Karim Residence, CRP, Interview, pp. 8–9.

The Star, Heeding Nature's Call, Malaysia, August 2006: p.15.

Daily Times Karachi, Pakistan Bangladesh Architect Urges Indus Valley Students to Go Green, November 2006: Meghna Residence, Karim Residence

Design + Architecture, D+A, Singapore, Issue 33, 2006: Profile on Rafiq Azam, Khazedewan Apartment, pp. 24–25.

2005

Il Progetto Dell'Abitare, Italy, April 2005: Khazedewan Apartment, pp. 33–41.

The Daily Star, Weekend Magazine, Bangladesh, Architect's Profile, April 8, 2005: Khazedewan Apartment, Haroon Residence, pp. 24–25.

2004

Architecture Asia, Journal of the Architects Regional Council Asia (Arcasia), Malaysia, Issue 2, June–August 2004: Karim Residence, pp. 18–21.

2003

Star City, The Daily Star, Bangladesh, July 9, 2003: Khazedewan Apartment

Probe, Bangladesh, vol. 2, Issue 15, August 1–16, 2003: Khazedewan Apartment

Architecture Asia, ARCASIA Journal (Architects Regional Council Asia), Malaysia, Issue 3, September–November 2003: Khazedewan Apartment, pp. 14–17.

2002

Architecture Asia, ARCASIA Journal, Malaysia, Issue 2, June 2002

Accolade, 2002: Haroon Residence (Apartment Building at Lalmatia), pp. 28–35.

SELECTED ONLINE PODCASTS

"Building Tomorrow with Ideas," Building Technology & Ideas Ltd., March 7, 2025

"Art of Negotiation: The Journey of Rafiq Azam," Diary of an Architectural Photographer, March 1, 2024

"Nandonik Nirmaner Golpo," Prothom Alo, November 24, 2024

"Building Tomorrow," Building Technology & Ideas Ltd., June 18, 2022

"Architect Rafiq Azam: Shatotto Injecting Life into Buildings," Design Story, July 2, 2020

"Design Conversations: Each Other Together, with Mustapha Khalid Palash & Md. Rafiq Azam," BRAC University, August 17, 2020

"Architecture for Green Living | Architecture in Bangladesh," BProperty Bites, July 10, 2019

SELECTED BANGLADESH TELEVISION

"Rafiq Azam & Zannat Jui," talk show, Masranga TV, September 20, 2024

"The Shadow of One Tree Is Equal to 30 ACs," Desh TV, April 26, 2024

"Nirman Roshayon," ATN News, July 30, 2023

"Rafiq Azam in Bunoner Golpo Show," Channel 9, July 19, 2022

"Architect Rafiq Azam Gets International Award for Rasulbagh Shishu Park," Ekattor TV, July 2022

"Robert Matthews Award," RTV News, July 13, 2022

"First Bangladeshi to Receive Robert Matthews Lifetime Achievement Award," Jamuna TV, July 9, 2022

"Uddipto Bangladesher Obhijatri: Rafiq Azam," *The Daily Star*, May 17, 2022

"Rafiq Azam & Zannat Jui," celebrity talk show, Channel 1, June 16, 2021

"300 Seconds," Channel 1, Ep. 493, March 8, 2021

"Shobuj Bhobishyoter Prottashay," Shah Cement, June 6, 2021

"Architect Rafiq Azam," Independent Television, September 16, 2018

"SA Graveyard," Berger Award, SA TV, September 16, 2018

"Architect Rafiq Azam Wins ARCASIA 2017 Award," SA TV, September 11, 2018

SELECTED ONLINE PUBLICATIONS & INTERVIEWS

"Amore/Omor Residence," www.archdaily.com, March, 2025

"Amore/Omor Residence," www.archidiaries.com, April 2025

"SA Residence," Architecture Lab, June 8, 2024

"SA Residence, South Water Caress," www.archdaily.com, August 2012

"SA Residence, South Water Caress," AEC Café Blogs, September 2012

"Rafiq Azam: Great Bengalis, SA Residence," www.contemporist.com

"SA Residence," www.archivol.com

"Profile of Rafiq Azam, South Water Garden, South Water Caress, Meghna Residence," www.architecturenewsplus.com

"Interview, Poetry and Mysticism in Architecture," www.architimes.com

"SA Residence," www.architectural.com

"Profile of Rafiq Azam," www.world–architects.com

"Interview," www.creativebangladesh.com

COMPLETED WORKS

1986–1988

Azam Residence, Lalbagh, Dhaka

1990

Beximco Pavilion at International Trade Fair, Dhaka

1990–1995

Drik Gallery, Dhanmondi, Dhaka

1994–1995

H.R.C Residence, Gulshan, Dhaka

1995–1996

Ena Residence, Gulshan, Dhaka

1995–1997

Niloy, Gulshan, Dhaka

Lake Side, Banani, Dhaka

White House, Baridhara, Dhaka

Gono Shasthya, Dhanmondi, Dhaka

1996–1997

Col. Rashid Residence, Cantonment, Dhaka

1996–1998

Silva Apartment, Gulshan, Dhaka

Accolade, Dhanmondi, Dhaka

Down Town, Mirpur, Dhaka

1997–1999

Yousuf Hassain Residence, Uttara, Dhaka

Dhanmondi Dell, Dhanmondi, Dhaka

Exclusive Circle, Gulshan, Dhaka

Swajan Apartment, Dhanmondi, Dhaka

Khurshid Garden, Gulshan, Dhaka

Forid Apartment, Gulshan, Dhaka

Green Villa, Gulshan, Dhaka

Farah Garden, Gulshan, Dhaka

Syed Ahmed Apartment, Uttara, Dhaka

1998–1999

Anwaruzzaman Residence, Gulshan, Dhaka

Harun Residence, Lalmatia, Dhaka

1998–2000

Khulshi Apartment, Khulshi, Chittagong

Beximco Bunglow, Savar, Dhaka

Nirjon, Banani, Dhaka

Candle Wood, Dhanmondi, Dhaka

1998–2003

C.R.P Hospital, Mirpur, Dhaka

1999–2001

Alfa Dream, Nasirabad, Chittagong

1999–2004

Mizan Residence, Gulshan, Dhaka

2000–2001

Community Center, Gulshan, Dhaka

Uttara Residence, Dhaka

2000–2002

Mahmud Residence, Uttara, Dhaka

Karim Residence, Gulshan, Dhaka

East Lake, Dhanmondi, Dhaka

Gulfeshan, Gulshan, Dhaka

2001–2002

Khazedewan Apartment, Lalbagh, Dhaka

2002–2004

South Wonder Apartment, Dhanmondi, Dhaka

2003–2005

Meghna Residence, Dhanmondi, Dhaka

2004–2006

Hill View Regency Apartment, Chittagong

2004–2007
South Water Garden, Baridhara, Dhaka

2005–2008
Bay Tower, Gulshan, Dhaka

2005–2011
SA Residence, Gulshan, Dhaka

2006–2008
Iqbal Apartment, DOHS Baridhara, Dhaka
Nilu Square Project, Satmosjid Road, Dhanmondi, Dhaka
Abul Khair Residence, D.T Road, Chittagong

2006–2009
Intraco Grand Villa, Baridhara, Dhaka

2006–2010
Mamun Residence, South Khulshi, Chittagong

2007–2008
Romana Roaf Chowdhury (interior), Rangs Waterfront, Gulshan, Dhaka

2007–2009
48 Park Road Apartment, Baridhara, Dhaka
Alif Breeze Apartment, Gulshan, Dhaka
Assurance Primrose Garden, Gulshan, Dhaka
Rangs Maloncha, Dhanmondi, Dhaka
Parveen (interior) Panchlaish, Chittagong

2007–2010
Equity Sylvestra, Khulshi, Chittagong
Intraco, Cantonment area, Chittagong

2007–2025
Bangladesh Chancery Complex, Islamabad, Pakistan

2008–2010
Rangs Grace Apartment, Gulshan, Dhaka

2008–2013
Shanta Nilambori, Banani, Dhaka

2009–2011
Abul Khair Residence, Chittagong
Arafin Residence, Gulshan, Dhaka
Navana Southern Wood, Dhanmondi, Dhaka
South Water Caress, Baridhara, Dhaka
Rangs Hena Dale, Gulshan, Dhaka

2009–2013
SA Taj Mahal, Noakhali
Assurance Cherry Blossom, Banani, Dhaka
Asset Development, Gulshan, Dhaka

2009–2014
Khaled Residence, Uttara, Dhaka

2010–2012
Akbar Hossain Residence, Uttara, Dhaka
Spl Malancha, Uttara, Dhaka
South Dew, Uttara, Dhaka
Tapas Residence, Banani, Dhaka

2010–2013
SA Paribahan Office, Chittagong
SA Paribahan Office, Khulna
SA Paribahan Office, Rangpur
South 50/53 Apartments, Gulshan, Dhaka
Zahir Paradise, Dhanmondi, Dhaka
Mahabub Alam Residence, Gulshan, Dhaka
Assurance Sangsaptak, Baridhara, Dhaka
Coral Reef Heritage, Cox's Bazaar
Equity Tillotoma, Chttiagong
Empori Apartment, Gulshan, Dhaka
Khurshid Jamil Residence, Khulshi, Chittagoing
Addl Lalkuthi, Lalmatia, Dhaka
Kishwar Jahan Residence, Banani, Dhaka
Equity Odyssey, Khulshi, Chittagong

2010–2014
South Anupam Apartment, Dhanmondi, Dhaka
South Proshanti Apartment, Dhanmondi, Dhaka
Huda's South Skyline, Gulshan, Dhaka
Assurance Dakshinayan, Dhanmondi, Dhaka
South Ruby's Blue Water, Dhanmondi, Dhaka

2010–2025
Bangladesh Chancery Complex, Thimpu, Bhutan

2011–2012
SA Family Graveyard, Noakhali

2011–2013
South Grace Apartment, Rajar Bazar, Dhaka
Sharia Sharmin Residence, Chandpur

2011–2014
South Symphony, Farmgate, Dhaka
Assurance Villa De Mahima, Gulshan, Dhaka
Equity Orchid, Khulshi, Chittagong
Empori Apartment, Gulshan, Dhaka
Omar Ali Residence, Cda Chittagong
Navana, 128 Gulshan, Dhaka

2011– 2015
Abul Hossain Residence, Chatteshwari, Chittagong

2011– 2016
South Huda's Skyline, Dhaka

2012–2014
SP Setia Headquarters, Kuala Lumpur, Malaysia
South Serenity, Gulshan, Dhaka

2012–2015
Coral Reef Sky Line, Cox's Bazaar
Spl Lading 141, Gulshan, Dhaka
Spl Babita, Gulshan, Dhaka
MA Hashem Residence, Gulshan, Dhaka
Imran Ur Rahman Residence, Uttara, Dhaka
Lakeside Lovely, Gulshan, Dhaka

2013–2015
Coral Reef Apartment, Cox's Bazaar
Azam Residence, Lalbagh, Dhaka
Arshad Jamal Residence, Nikunja, Dhaka
Majumder Arif Residence, Bashundhara, Dhaka
Ashraf Kaiser Residence, Savar, Dhaka

2013–2016
Bhuyan Bari, Khilkhet, Dhaka
Ruby's Blue Water, Dhanmondi, Dhaka
South Garden Apartment, Baridhara, Dhaka
South Shama, Baridhara, Dhaka
Bio Cox's Palace, Cox's Bazaar
Spl 13/A Dhanmondi, Dhaka
Addl, 32 Dhanmondi, Dhaka
Shakti Foundation for Disadvantaged, Mirpur, Dhaka
Captain Ahmedul Kabir Residence, Banani, Dhaka
Swargio Dutabash, Baridhara, Dhaka
Ibory Builders. Bashundhara, Dhaka
Dipu Sharmin Residence

2013–2017
Assurance Aporajeyo, Dhanmondi, Dhaka
Idris Shakur Residence, Baridhara, Dhaka
South Basera Breeze Apartment, Baridhara, Dhaka

2014–2016
Rokia Afzal Vacation House, Gazipur
Hamid Group, 09 Banani, Dhaka
Pfi Properties, Plot 32, Niketon, Dhaka
Pfi Properties, 2-A Banani, Dhaka
Ashfaq Residence, Shyamoli, Dhaka

2014–2017
South Leaf Apartment, Gulshan, Dhaka
South Serenity Apartment, Gulshan, Dhaka
South Basera Apartment, Baridhara, Dhaka
South Majesty Apartment, Dhanmondi, Dhaka
Bio, Dhanmondi, Dhaka
Ibrahim Consortium, Gulshan, Dhaka
Eastern Housing, Paribagh, Dhaka
Hamid Group, 01 Banani, Dhaka
Partex Properties, New Eskaton, Dhaka
Jumairah May Flower, Amirbag, Chittagong

2014–2018
Equity Arunima, Chawk Bazaar, Chittagong
Spl 18, Banani, Dhaka
Spl 66, Gulshan, Dhaka
Spl 16, Banani, Dhaka
Pfi Properties, Gulshan, Dhaka
Azherul Islam Residence, Gulshan, Dhaka

2015–2018
Ddc, Gulshan, Dhaka
Urmi Group, Banani, Dhaka

2015–2020
Spl Debonair, Dhaka

2015–2022
Us-Bangla Master Plan, Rampura, Dhaka

2016–2018
Mayor Hanif Jame Mosque, Azimpur, Dhaka

2017–2019
Abashik City—Bijoy Niketon, Posogola, Dhaka
Bahadur Shah Park, Lalbagh, Dhaka
Shahid Abdul Alim Playground, Lalbagh, Dhaka

2017–2020
Bahadur Shah Park, Dhaka
Asif Zahir Residence, Gulshan, Dhaka

2017–2021
Haque's South Leaf, Gulshan, Dhaka

2017–2022
Aga Khan Academy, Dhaka

2018–2021
Rasulbagh Shishu Park, Lalbagh, Dhaka

2018–2024
Delowar Hossain Area Development, Dhaka

2018–ongoing
Osmani Udyan, Dhaka

2019–2024
Shadhin Residence, Basundhara, Dhaka

2020–2023
Azimpur Public Restrooms, Dhaka

UNBUILT WORKS

Design Period, 2005–2006
Newaz Residence

Design Period, 2009
SA Village Home
Dillish Residence, Chennai, India
Emtazul Islam Residence, Chandra Nagar, Chittagong
Anbis Development, Sutrapur, Dhaka
Anbis Development, Genderia, Dhaka
Eastern Eco Village, Mirpur, Dhaka

Design Period, 2010
Lot 3, Kuala Lumpur, Malaysia
Lot 12, Kuala Lumpur, Malaysia
Lot 13, Kuala Lumpur, Malaysia
Lot 14, Kuala Lumpur, Malaysia
Lot 15, Kuala Lumpur, Malaysia

Design Period, 2011
Equity Wajihun Bag Residence, Panchlaish, Chittagong
Paathshala Institute, Panthapath, Dhaka

Design Period, 2011
Equity Wajihun Bag Residence, Panchlaish, Chittagong
Pathshala Institute, Panthapath, Dhaka

Design Period, 2012
Abul Hossain Residence, Gulshan, Dhaka
Abul Khair Residence, Savar, Dhaka
Dhaka Club, Dhaka
Oj Residence, Sylhet
Us-Bangla School, Rampura, Dhaka

FEATURED WORKS (order of appearance)

SA RESIDENCE (2005–2011)
Type: Single-Family Residence
Land Area: 1,112 m^2
Built Area: 1,920 m^2
Client: Salahuddin Ahmed
Principal Architect: Rafiq Azam
Assistant Principal Architect: Md. Akter Hossen
Project Engineer: Md. Akter Hossen and Khorshed Alam Shamim
Civil Contractors: Shah Alam
Structural Engineer: Md. Shamsul Alam
Plumbing and Mechanical Engineer: Md. Sayedul Islam.
Electrical Engineer: Md. Lutfor Rahman
Landscape: Prof. Rafiq Azam (FIAB) and Kaji Kanchon
Paintings: Syed Hasan Mahmud

AGA KHAN ACADEMY (Phase 1 2017–2022)
Type: Educational Institution
Land Area: 74,150 m^2
Built Area: 40,000 m^2
Client: Aga Khan Academy
Consultants: Shatotto and Feilden Clegg Bradley Studios
Principal Architects: Rafiq Azam and Peter Clegg
Design Team: Sabrin Zinat Rahman, Kaiser Rabbani, Arafat Sarker, Sonia Redwan, Fayez Aliza, Shylin Islam
FCB Studios: Peter Clegg, Ian Taylor, Felix Hobson, Rachel Sayers, Jo Gimenez
Resident Architect: Edrish Bhuiyan Almas
Brick Consultant: Mahmudul Hasan Nahid, Mehedi Hasan Prince.
Structural Consultant: AKT- II, TDM
MEP Consultant: Max Fordham & EMCS
Landscape Consultant: Shatotto and Ghorami Jon
Contractor: Charuta Private Limited

DIPU SHARMIN RESIDENCE (2013–2016)
Type: Residential
Land Area: 401.13 m^2
Built Area: 259.10 m^2
Client: Shamima Sharmin and Arshad Jamal Dipu
Principal Architect: Rafiq Azam
Design Team: Sabrin Zinat Rahman
Supervision Engineer: Shaju
Interior: Sharmin and River & Rain
Landscape: Shatotto, Sharmin, and River & Rain

ASIF ZAHIR RESIDENCE (2017– 2020)
Type: Residential
Land Area: 608.51 m^2
Built Area: 419.92 m^2
Client: Asif Zahir
Principal Architect: Rafiq Azam
Design Team: Md. Mahmudul Haque, Nilufar Yasmin Neela, Md. Naimul Islam
Structural Engineer: Md. Asaduzzaman

HAQUE'S SOUTH LEAF (2017–2021)
Type: Residential
Land Area:1370 m^2
Built Area: 946 m^2
Client: South Breeze Housing Ltd.
Principal Architect: Rafiq Azam
Design Team: Sabrin Zinat Rahman, Mehanaz Sultana, Ahasan Akter Shohag
(3D Visualizer)
Construction Head: Md. Akter Hossen

SHADHIN RESIDENCE (2019–2024)
Type: Residential
Land Area: 670 m^2
Built area: 435 m^2
Client: A.K.M Azad Shadhin
Principal Architect: Rafiq Azam
Design Team: Zannat Jui, Tohidul Islam
Supervision Engineer: Md. Akter Hossen

SP SETIA HEADQUARTERS (2012–2014)

Type: Office Building

Land Area: 12,300 m^2

Built Area: 33,838 m^2

Client: Bandar Setia Alam Sdn Bhd

Principal Architect: Rafiq Azam

Design Team: Shatotto, Sihaam Shaheed, Nubaira Haque Shipa, Archicentre Sdn Bhd-Ng Hai Yean, Ms. Inthirani

Civil Contractors: Santarli Sdn Bhd-Johny Choong and Jason Low

Civil and Structural Engineer: Tylin International Sdn Bhd-Sia Pie King and Robin Yip, Weng Cheong

Mechanical and Electrical Engineer: Ssp (E&M) Sdn Bhd-Ooi Chee Wee and Lam Kai Min

Quantity Surveyor: Bahaduruddin Ali and Low Sdn Bhd-Eddie Chin Pak Hoe and Wong Chee Leong

Gbi Facilitator: Greenspaces Sdn Bhd-David Ong Yaw Hian

Landscape Designer: Shatotto, Rafiq Azam, Landarc Associates – Lee Kwai Pheng

BANGLADESH CHANCERY COMPLEX BHUTAN (2010–2025)

Type: Government Institution

Land Area: 6,072 m^2

Built Area: 6,052.95 m^2

Client: Embassy of the People's Republic of Bangladesh in Thimphu, Bhutan

Design Consultant: Shatotto

Principal Architect: Rafiq Azam, in association with Progressive Research & Consultancy Services (Bhutan), Ideas Pty Ltd & Iftekhar+ Design Associates (Australia)

Design Team: Tohidul Islam, Rebecca, Sabrin Zinat Rahman, Nurun Nahar, Nazrul Islam, Md. Akter Hossen, Afsara Tasnim

Construction Team: Vajra Builders Pvt. Ltd (Bhutan)

Structural Engineer: M.P Nepal, Kiwan Nath Siwakoti

Supervision Engineer: Md. Oahedul Islam

Electrical Engineer: Md. Mohiminol Islam

Mechanical & Plumbing Engineer: EMCS

MAYOR MOHAMMAD HANIF JAME MOSQUE (2016–2018)

Type: Religious Center

Land Area: 1,427.08 m^2

Built Area: 1,207.83 m^2

Client: Dhaka South City Corporation (DSCC)

Principal Architect: Rafiq Azam

Design Team: Ikramoon Nisa, Ibtesa Moon Adittya, Mehnaz Sultana and Prince, Nahid (Studio D'Void)

Supervision Engineer: Md. Lutfor Rahman, Md. Akter Hossen

Structural Engineer: Mustafizur Rahman

Electrical Engineer: Md. Mohiminol Islam

AZIMPUR PUBLIC RESTROOMS (2020–2023)

Type: Public Amenity

Land Area: 98.37 m^2

Built Area: 70.40 m^2

Client: Dhaka South City Corporation (DSCC)

Principal Architect: Rafiq Azam

Design Team: Savyasachi Mondal, Rehnuma Tasnim Sheefa, Jouairia Hossain Mou

Supervision Engineer: Md. Lutfor Rahman

Structural Engineer: Md. Akter Hossen

BAHADUR SHAH PARK (2017–2019)

Type: Revitalization

Land Area: 3,600 m^2

Client: Dhaka South City Corporation (DSCC)

Principal Architect: Rafiq Azam

Design Team: Adhora, Arifur Rahman, Jouairia Hossain Mou, Anika Asif, Bejury Ansary

Structural Engineer: Md. Lutfor Rahman

Electrical Engineer: Md. Mohiminol Islam

DELOWAR HOSSAIN AREA DEVELOPMENT (2018–2024)

Type: Revitalization

Land Area: 6,532 m^2

Built Area: 6,532 m^2

Client: Dhaka South City Corporation (DSCC)

Principal Architect: Rafiq Azam

Design Team: Audhora Sharmin, Ariful Rahman Kaushik, Bejury Ansary, Suraktim, Saiprasanth, Rishad Amlani, Hashim Reza, Khairul Islam, Md. Kamrul Alam

Supervision Engineer: Md. Lutfor Rahman

Structural Engineer: MD Akter Hossen, Nazrul Islam

Electrical Engineer: Md. Mohiminol Islam

RASULBAGH SHISHU PARK (2018–2021)

Type: Revitalization

Land Area: 2,848 m^2

Gross internal floor area: 346.69 m^2

Client: Dhaka South City Corporation (DSCC)

Principal Architect: Rafiq Azam

Design Team: Audhora Sharmin, Ariful Rahman Kaushik, Bejury Ansary, Suraktim, Saiprasanth, Rishad Amlani, Hashim Reza, Khairul Islam,, Md. Kamrul Alam

Supervision Engineer: Md. Lutfor Rahman

Structural Engineer: MD Akter Hossen, Nazrul Islam

Electrical Engineer: Md. Mohiminol Islam

OSMANI UYDAN (2018–ongoing)

Type: Revitalization

Land Area: 99,868 m^2

Client: Dhaka South City Corporation (DSCC)

Consultant: Shatotto and JPZ (JV)

Principal Architect: Rafiq Azam

Design Team: Sihaam Saheed, Bejury Ansary, Mahedi Hassan Rijon, Md. Kamrul Alam (3D visualizer)

Supervision Engineer: Md. Elias Miah, Md. Lutfor Rahman

Structural Engineer: Shatotto and JPZ (JV)

Landscape Designer: Shatotto and JPZ (JV)

Electrical Engineer: Md. Mohiminol Islam and Shams Engineering

CURRENT EMPLOYEES

Aaraf Dayad Azam
Bejury Ansary
Edrish Bhuiyan Almas
Humayun Ahmed Himu
Jamal Hossain Shaon
Mahedi Hassan Rijon
Mahiyat Mubassera
Mahmudul Hasan
Md. Abdullah Parvez
Md. Kamrul Alam
Md. Mahabubur Rahman Mokter
Md. Mahafuzur Rahman
Md. Mohiminol Islam
Md. Zahid Hossain
Mifta Uddin Ushan
Md. Lutfor Rahman
Md. Shahjahan Kabir
Zannat Jui
Nurun Nahar Lopa
Parveen Khan
Ruhul Amin
Samiha Sultana
Sihaam Shaheed
Sultan Mahamood
Sumaiya Sarwat
Tohidul Islam
Lamia Latif
Md. Arafat Hossain
Md Azizur Rahman
Md. Mostafijur Rahman (Shuvo)
Snigdha Arzoo

FORMER EMPLOYEES

A. Mannan Khan
ASM. Mehedi Hasan
Abdullah Al Hossain Chowdhury
Abdullah Al Masud
Afroza Akter Nila
Afruzzaman Khan
Afsana Luqman
Ahasan Akter
Aminul Hassan
Antara Mohima Baroi
Antara Talukdar
Arup Kumar Das
Ashraful Kawser
Asma Khan
Farah Naz
Farhana Tasneem
Farjan Akter
Faruq Hossain
Halima Rahman
Iqra Binte Zamil
Istiak Ahmed
Jaharia Ferdaws Tushi
Jamal Uddin Bhuiyan
Kaiser Rabbany Rabbi
Kamal Hosain
Kazi Shamima Sharmin
Kazi Touhid Elahi
Khairul Islam
Khandokar Zakaria
Mahamudul Hasan Sabbir
Mamunur Rashid
Marhana Susan
Mashud Hasan
Md. Abu Sayed
Md. Ahshan Habib
Md. Aman
Md. Ashraful Kawser
Md. Azgar Sarder
Md. Elias Miah
Md. Giash Uddin Zia
Md. Habib Khan
Md. Iqbal Hossen
Md. Mainuddin
Md. Masudur Rahman
Md. Mizanur Rahman
Md. Monasur Rahman
Md. Monwer Hossain
Md. Nazrul Islam
Md. Nizam Uddin Thakur
Md. Roushon-ul-Islam
Md. Saha Alam
Md. Tanjimur Rahman
Md. Ziaur Rahman
Md. Akter Hossen
Moynul Hassan
Moynul Hossain
Nahida Akbar
Nahidul Islam
Nasima Khan
Nishat Afrose
Nubaira Hoque Shipa
Nurun Nahar Lopa
Nusrat Wahid
Rahmatul Aziz
Rebeka Sultana
Rezaul Asad
Rima Fariaz
Rokeya Begum
Safiqul Islam
Saiful Islam
Saima Begum
Salahuddin Chowdhury
Shaheen Akhter
Shakir Azim Ullah
Sharfun Nahar
Sharmin Akter
Shohidul Islam
Sk. Samimul Haque
Sohel Iqbal
Sonia Chowdhury
Sonia Guha
Syed Shahjahan Sagar
Takdir Bepari
William Bonowary
Yassir Sanjari
Zannatul Ferdouse Ahona
Afsara Tasnim
Anika Asif
Arafat Sarker
Ariful Rahman Kaushik
Audhora Sharmin26. Hashim Reza
Ibtesa Moon Adittya
Ikramoon Nisa
Jouairia Hossain Mou
Mantasha Abdullah
Md. Mahmudul Haque
Md. Naimul Islam
Mehnaz Sultana
Nazrul Islam
Nishat Afrose
Rehnuma Tasnim Sheefa
Rishad Amlani
Sabrin Zinat Rahman
Sabrina Mehjabeen Ratree
Saiprasanth
Samar Matabbar
Savyasachi Mondal
Shylin Islam
Sonia Redwan
Suraktim

ACKNOWLEDGMENTS

Shatotto extends its gratitude to the architects, project owners, and families, who graciously allowed us to feature their work and homes in this book. We also want to express our appreciation to all our conscientious staff in Dhaka and elsewhere for their invaluable efforts and contributions. Your work is a source of hope and inspiration for a peaceful and sustainable future.

Working on this book has been an important touchstone for me personally, but it also reaffirms the energy of practicing architects, urban planners, and clients in this region, who are overcoming challenges and achieving great objectives.

I especially thank Rosa Maria Falvo, my long-standing editor, and Giorgio Gardel, who have demonstrated their unwavering support and expertise to produce this high-quality book. Our gratitude also extends to the rest of the Rizzoli team in Milan, who believed in this project and its place in a more balanced survey of global architecture.

We also recognize the crucial role that government, foundations, and organizations play in funding new development and research that pave the way for progress.

We extend our gratitude to the contributors, who were essential to the realization of this book: Kenneth Brian Frampton CBE, Shamsul Wares, Fuad H. Mallick, Rosa Maria Falvo, Philip Goad, and George Kunihiro. They each generously gave their time and expertise to this project.

I owe my career and this book to all those who have supported and guided me over the years. I sincerely thank the partners of SHATOTTO architecture for green living—especially my wife, Ar. Zannat Jui, Associate Principal Architect, along with Sihaam Shaheed, Md. Kamrul Alam, and Tohidul Islam—for their dedicated leadership and unwavering commitment.

I would like to especially thank Dr. Tan Loke Mun, my design partner from Malaysia, whose support and assistance have been truly invaluable. I would also like to express my appreciation for all those who have directly or indirectly taken an interest in promoting my book in Australia, Africa, Bhutan, China, UAE, England, France, Germany, India, Indonesia, Italy, Japan, Malaysia, Pakistan, Portugal, Russia, Singapore, Sri Lanka, Spain, Thailand, USA, and Vietnam.

I express my sincere gratitude to Ar. Asijit Khan, from India, for mentoring our team in Dhaka and his incredible dedication that helped shape the book. I would also like to thank artist Syed Hasan Mahmud for offering his constant support and critiques. My heartfelt thanks to Samiha Sultana, Mahiyat Mubassera, and Lamia Latif for their constant diligence.

I extend special thanks to my son, Aaraf, and my daughter, Juwayriya, whose constant motivation and encouragement inspire me to keep doing meaningful work.
I am deeply grateful to my father-in-law, Dr. Zahid Hossain, and my mother-in-law, Surma Zahid, for ensuring everything ran smoothly in my absence.

I am still on a journey of learning—continuously seeking knowledge and growth to better myself, both as an architect and as a human being. My purpose goes beyond designing buildings; it is rooted in the desire to uplift lives by creating spaces that nurture the soul and inspire hope. Through architecture, I strive to spread positivity, foster well-being, and contribute to a more meaningful and beautiful future for people and the communities they live in.

IMAGE CREDITS

Asif Salman, pp. 34, 46, 48-51, 54-56, 59-61, 78-80, 86-89, 94, 97, 98, 110-111, 114-116, 144, 273, 286, 290-291, 294, 297-301
City Syntax, pp. 122-139, 146, 198, 200-201, 224-225, 250-251, 254- 256, 260-269, 280-281, 284-285, 287, 289, 292-293
Prantography, pp. 92-93, 104-107, 212-221, 274, 304-305
Maruf Raihan, pp. 228, 231, 233, 236-237
Protick Sarker, pp. 40-41, 47, 52-53, 118-119
Hassan Saifuddin Chandan, pp. 12, 65, 82, 84-85
FCB Studios, p. 45
Md. Kamrul Alam and Tohidul Islam, pp. 168-169,176-179
Md. Kamrul Alam, pp. 306, 308-309, 312-317
Bejury Ansary, pp. 17, 243
Md. Rafiq Azam, pp. 13, 150-156, 161,173-175
Zannat Jui, pp. 166-167, 170, 226, 234-235, 247
Rosa Maria Falvo, pp. 72-73, 183-185, 188
Mike Kelley, pp. 96, 101-103, 196-197, 204-209, 241, 244
Daniele Domenicali, pp. 13, 20-29, 33
H Lin Ho, pp. 14, 158-160, 162-163
Choton Haque, p. 112
Will Scott, pp. 202-203
Abdul Momin, pp. 42
Shatotto Historical Archive, pp. 66, 145, 190-191, 230, 232, 252, 272, 276-279, 287, 295, 296
Paul Marvin Rudolph Archive, Library of Congress, p. 64
Flickr Abrinsky (CC BY-NC-SA), p. 64
Georges Chevalier (CC BY 4.0), p. 71
Jyotirindranath Tagore, Indian National Museum, p. 74
Nacása & Partners Inc., p.142
indianculture.gov.in_Dikhsit,Rao Bahadur K.N.6, p.143

CONTRIBUTORS

KENNETH B. FRAMPTON

Kenneth B. Frampton trained as an architect at the Architectural Association School of Architecture, London. He has taught at a number of leading institutions in the field, including the Royal College of Art in London, the ETH in Zürich, the Berlage Institute in Amsterdam, EPFL in Lausanne, and the Accademia di Architettura in Mendrisio. From 1972 to 2019, he served as Ware Professor of Architecture at the Graduate School of Architecture, Planning and Preservation at Columbia University, New York. He is the author of numerous essays on modern and contemporary architecture, has served on many international juries for architectural awards and building commissions, and is a member of the American Academy of Arts and Letters. In 2018, he was awarded the Golden Lion of the Venice Biennale. His publications include *Studies in Tectonic Culture* (1992), *Labour, Work and Architecture* (2005), *American Masterworks* (2008), *Kengo Kuma: Complete Works* (2012), and *A Genealogy of Modern Architecture* (2013). He was awarded the British Honour of CBE in 2021 and the Jefferson Medal of Architecture from the University of Virginia in 2022.

SHAMSUL WARES

Professor Shamsul Wares is an esteemed Bangladeshi architect and educator. Graduating from Bangladesh University of Engineering and Technology (BUET) in 1968, he served as a faculty member there from 1972 to 2003 and has since been a professor of architecture at the University of Asia Pacific in Dhaka. Wares began his architectural practice working under the renowned architect Muzharul Islam early in his career (1968–1971). He has held significant leadership roles, including two terms as the president of the Institute of Architects Bangladesh (IAB) from 1997–1999 and 1995–1997. He has been a member of international juries for architectural awards and competitions, such as the Architect of the Year Award, CAA 7th and 9th International Student Design Competitions (2006 and 2013), and the ARCASIA Award for Architecture. He has participated in various international seminars and lectures and represented Bangladesh in ARCASIA Council Meetings. In recognition of his contributions to architectural education, Wares received the Lifetime Achievement Award from the IAB in 2009.

FUAD H. MALLICK

Fuad Hassan Mallick is a distinguished professor and Dean of the School of Architecture and Design at BRAC University. He has been teaching and researching architecture for over thirty years in Bangladesh and abroad. He has a Bachelor of Architecture from the Bangladesh University of Engineering and Technology (BUET), and M.Phil. in Housing Studies from the University of Newcastle upon Tyne, UK, and a PhD in Environment and Energy Studies Program from the Architectural Association Graduate School in London. Professor Mallick has conducted pioneering research on thermal comfort for Bangladesh and published extensively on this subject. He is the founder of the Department of Architecture of BRAC University and the leading author of its curriculum. He is also the founding director of the university's postgraduate programs in Disaster Management, the first of its kind in the region. His research interests focus on the environmental aspects of architectural design, low income and rural housing, architectural education, and disaster management and climate change.

ROSA MARIA FALVO

Rosa Maria Falvo is an accomplished writer, editor, and curator in Milan and Melbourne, specializing in Asia Pacific and Middle Eastern contemporary art and design. She graduated with an Honours Degree of Bachelor of Arts (First Class) and a Diploma of Education (English Literature and Biology) from Monash University in Melbourne, Australia. After her first career as a leading teacher, she began traveling and later studied European avant-garde art at Perugia University in Italy. For over 20 years, Rosa has published widely, working closely with artists, writers, galleries, collectors, foundations, corporations, and cultural bodies in the production and promotion of art books and exhibition projects. She is the editor of *Rafiq Azam: Architecture for Green Living*, Skira Editore, Milan (2013). Rosa has been a guest presenter at numerous venues, including the Chobi Mela International Photo Festival and Dhaka Art Summit in Bangladesh, Fotografie Museum in Amsterdam; Foreign Correspondents' Club in Tokyo, Shanghai & Beijing M Literary Festivals, India Art Fair Global Forum, Oxford Centre for Islamic Studies in Oxford; and the American Institute of Architects in New York.

PHILIP GOAD

Philip Goad is Chair of Architecture, Redmond Barry Distinguished Professor, and co-director of the Australian Centre for Architectural History, Urban and Cultural Heritage (ACAHUCH) at the University of Melbourne. He is a former President of the Australian Institute of Architects (Victorian Chapter) and the Society of Architectural Historians of Australia, New Zealand (SAHANZ). He is a Life Fellow of the Australian Institute of Architects (LFRAIA) and a Fellow of the Australian Academy of the Humanities (FAHA). He is co-editor of *The Encyclopedia of Australian Architecture*, Cambridge University Press, UK, 2012 and *Australia Modern: Architecture, Landscape & Design, 1925–1975*, Thames & Hudson Australia (2019). His writings on contemporary architecture in South and Southeast Asia include contributions to *Architecture Bali* (2000), *New Directions in Tropical Asian Architecture* (2005), and *Rafiq Azam: Architecture for Green Living*, Skira Editore, Milan (2013). He contributed the entry on "Southeast Asia, Australasia and Oceania, 1900–2020" in Murray Fraser (ed.), *Sir Banister Fletcher's Global History of Architecture*, Bloomsbury Press, UK, 2018.

GEORGE KUNIHIRO

George Kunihiro is a prominent American architect and educator with a global influence. He graduated from UC Berkeley, earned a Master of Architecture from Harvard, and completed his PhD course at the University of Tokyo. Kunihiro was a Professor of Architecture at Kokushikan University in Tokyo (1998–2022) and has been a Visiting Professor at Tsinghua University in Beijing since 2011. He has also taught at leading institutions including Yale, Columbia, Harvard, and NJIT. Kunihiro has held significant leadership roles, including President of the Architectural Regional Council Asia (ARCASIA) and various positions within the American Institute of Architects (AIA). He has received numerous international awards, including Presidential Medals from the AIA and the Federación de Colegios de Arquitectos de México, and is a Richard Upjohn Fellow of the AIA. Kunihiro has also served on architectural design juries in several countries, contributing extensively to the field of architecture.

Shatotto

Design Curator
Asijit Khan

Layout and illustrations
Aaraf Dayad Azam
Samiha Sultana
Tanvir Harunor
Tulika Mondal Megha

Creative Advisor
Syed Hasan Mahmud

Rizzoli

Editor
Rosa Maria Falvo

Art Director
Giorgio Gardel

Distributed in English throughout the World by
Rizzoli International Publications, Inc.
49 West 27th Street
New York, NY 10001
www.rizzoliusa.com

ISBN: 978-88-918-3440-9

Printed in Italy
2025 2026 2027 2028 / 10 9 8 7 6 5 4 3 2 1

The authorized representative in the EU for product safety and compliance is Mondadori Libri S.p.A., via Gian Battista Vico 42, Milan, Italy, 20123, www.mondadori.it

Visit us online:
Instagram.com/RizzoliBooks
Facebook.com/RizzoliNewYork
Youtube.com/user/RizzoliNY